An Experience of LOVE

An Experience of LOVE

Understanding Natural Family Planning

Ingrid Trobisch
Elisabeth Roetzer

Fleming H. Revell Company
Old Tappan, New Jersey

An Experience of Love was first published in German under the title MIT FREUDEN FRAU SEIN 2 © 1977 Ingrid Trobisch and Elisabeth Roetzer.

Unless otherwise identified, Scripture quotations in this volume are from the King James Version of the Bible.

Scripture quotations identified RSV are from the Revised Standard Version of the Bible, copyrighted 1946, 1952, © 1971 and 1973.

Library of Congress Cataloging in Publication Data

Trobisch, Ingrid Hult.
An experience of love.

Translation of: Mit Freuden Frau sein 2.
1. Natural family planning. I. Roetzer, Elisabeth.
II. Title.
RG136.5.T7613 613.9′434 81-8651
ISBN 0-8007-1184-X AACR2

Published by Fleming H. Revell Company

Printed in the United States of America

TO couples who have the courage to
take the high road of love that
this book describes

Contents

Foreword

When my wife's book *The Joy of Being a Woman—And What a Man Can Do* (Harper & Row: New York, 1975) was published a few years ago, we had no idea that the bulk of our reader response would concern chapter 3, "Living in Harmony with the Cycle and Fertility." Here was something new and exciting to our readers. They wanted to make it a part of their lives, but none knew where to turn for practical advice.

The chapter contained, of course, only a few highlights relating to natural family planning as a way of life, for its purpose was to entice married couples to consider the possibility of living and growing together in harmony with their own fertility. We were simply amazed at how many of them were only too happy and thankful to take up this gentle suggestion. And yet, as their letters indicated, they really needed more information and practical instruction.

A lively correspondence developed and began to demand a great deal of my wife's time. And so, like Simon Peter when his net was breaking from the great catch of fish, she called out to "the other boat" for help and, with permission, sent a portion of the correspondence to our dear friend and adviser, Dr. Josef Roetzer, who lived not far from us. Dr.

Roetzer has pursued his investigations of the menstrual cycle for thirty years and is rightly considered one of the world's authorities in this field.

With the exemplary care and patience so evident in the following pages, Dr. Roetzer took upon himself the task of responding to our readers' questions, which in some cases meant continuing correspondence over a lengthy period of time. Eventually the demands of this task, in addition to his own correspondence, became so time-consuming that he in turn called upon another partner, his daughter Elisabeth (who at the time was working toward a degree in theology), to help him. Elisabeth has become her father's "right-hand man" in the evaluation and interpretation of more than 15,000 charted cycles and in compiling the data for scientific purposes.

But we must introduce yet a fourth partner in this effort: Dr. Rudolf Vollman, Ob./Gyn., an American physician now living in Switzerland. Dr. Vollman's pioneering work *The Menstrual Cycle* (W. B. Saunders: Philadelphia, 1977) has already won the solid respect of the American medical profession. Dr. Vollman, who introduced into medical literature the concept of gynecological age in women, is, as far as we know, the only physician in the world who has continuous records on the menstrual cycle, basal body temperature, intermenstrual pain, and cervical mucus over the entire reproductive lifetime of many women.

An Experience of Love is the result of the collaboration between my wife, Dr. Roetzer, his daughter Elisabeth, and Dr. Vollman. The reader will find here not a textbook, but a workbook; not a finished home, but a busy center, where one may peer over the shoulders of counselors with their clients, learn firsthand about their questions and needs, and muster courage to draw the appropriate conclusions. The reader will be challenged to take an active part in the further investigation of this frontier territory.

The readers who asked the questions are every bit as much the authors of this book as those who responded to their letters of inquiry. The correspondence has in part been so arranged that one reader enters into dialogue with another, though neither has ever met the other. Those providing the answers learn from those who posed the questions, and the important information thereby made available can in turn be communicated to an even wider audience. We see a group of pioneers emerging from this mutual give-and-take, who are embarking upon a new venture into the wonders of God's creation.

The correspondence in this book has been divided into sections reflecting a variety of typical circumstances and the most frequent questions relating to them. Chapter and subdivision headings provide easy orientation. A certain amount of repetition was necessary in order to make each case readily understandable and complete in itself. The correspondence consists of real letters to and from real people, who wrote down their own problems exactly as they appear here and who have graciously permitted the publication of their private correspondence.

Three things are obvious from these letters:

1. An amazing variety of living conditions and learning processes come into play: from the fifteen-year-old girl who wishes she could take her cycle and blast it into outer space, to the mature young woman who drops to her knees to adore the Creator when she ponders the miraculous pattern of events in her cycle of fertility.

One reader would like to see my wife's book burned, because he believes the sympto-thermal method is unreliable. Another author feels cheated because she has no grandchildren yet and is angry at my wife for providing a method of family planning that is too reliable. A third reader, a very pious lady, tries to make a case for the calendar-rhythm method of family planning, precisely because this outmoded method is so unreliable and therefore "at least gives God a chance."

The conflict of opinions reveals how inept we still are when confronted with the fact of our own fertility. This book takes the reader step-by-step along the path to a new understanding and appreciation of fertility.

2. The way of life proposed in the following pages is a noble one. Here we stand on holy ground. To allow new life to begin is intimate cooperation with God, a sacred trust coupled with personal responsibility. Here there is no room for superficiality. It is a matter of earnest and exacting precision, for we are dealing with the affirmation of one's own physical body. Beyond this step of self-acceptance lies a renewed reverence for one's own creatureliness, as well as a new love and awareness for the Creator.

3. The new way proposed here wells up from a deep, unshakable affirmation of life. When one stops to think that, in America, one-fourth of all couples in their fertile years have allowed themselves to be sterilized, then we understand the uneasy verdict of Solzhenitsyn when he says: "The West has lost its will to live."

This book will help us to find it again.

WALTER TROBISCH

Publisher's Note: Pastor Trobisch wrote this Foreword before his death on October 13, 1979.

1

What Is Natural Family Planning?

Natural family planning takes advantage of the biological fact that women are infertile most of the time during the reproductive years of their lives. This knowledge, together with planned abstinence, can be used either to achieve or avoid conception.

Couples facing their responsibility of parenting must engage in a dialogue leading to the choice of a way of life. This involves more than just the choice of a family-planning technique. Our purpose in natural family planning is not to tell people whether or not they should have children or how many they should have. Rather it is to provide couples with the information they need, so that their decisions—whether to achieve or avoid pregnancy—will be based on a learned awareness of the natural fertility cycle.

When Is Conception Possible?

Conception can occur only on a few days of the menstrual cycle. Most of the days of the cycle are infertile because the narrow canal leading through the cervix (the neck of the uterus) is closed, and therefore upward sperm migration is impossible. For that simple reason, it is only when the following changes have occurred that conception is possible:

- The narrow canal in the cervix has become wider.
- Increased secretion of a thin, watery fluid (mucus) from the widened cervix has made it possible for sperm to travel upward into the uterus. In the absence of this thin, watery-mucus, the sperm die within a few hours in the vagina.

This increase of watery mucus flows out through the vagina. It may be noticed at the vaginal entrance simply as a feeling of wetness—an increased secretion very different from a constant vaginal discharge. This increased *mucus secretion,* a sign of the fertile days, usually begins a few days before ovulation, therefore giving sufficient advance notice of an impending possible ovulation. The secretion is sometimes noticed immediately after the menstrual period, sometimes a few days after menstruation. When a particularly long cycle is developing, it won't be noticed until several days after menstruation. That is why personal self-observation is so very important—even more important than temperature taking during the early part of the cycle.

In the third world, a skilled teacher of natural family planning begins with the simple statement: "When I feel nothing at the vaginal opening, I am infertile. As soon as I notice *mucus sensations,* and for three days afterwards, I am fertile. From the fourth day after the mucus has ended, I know I am infertile." It seems to be easier for these women to observe their symptoms than for some American and European women, who may be desensitized by the clothing they wear—tight jeans, synthetic underwear, and the like. This awareness is the first step to self-knowledge in learning to live in harmony with one's fertility.

As the learning process continues, self-observation will gradually reveal further differences in the sensation and secretion at the vaginal opening. Forced, or strained, self-observation is not at all necessary. You must wait patiently until certain differences show up by themselves. Use an **M** (for **M**ucus) to record days of mucus secretion on your chart. *Mucus days* are considered fertile.

Before we tell you more details about self-observation, let us look at what happens during the cycle:

The Sequence of the Menstrual Cycle
M-P = menstrual period
O = potential *days* of ovulation

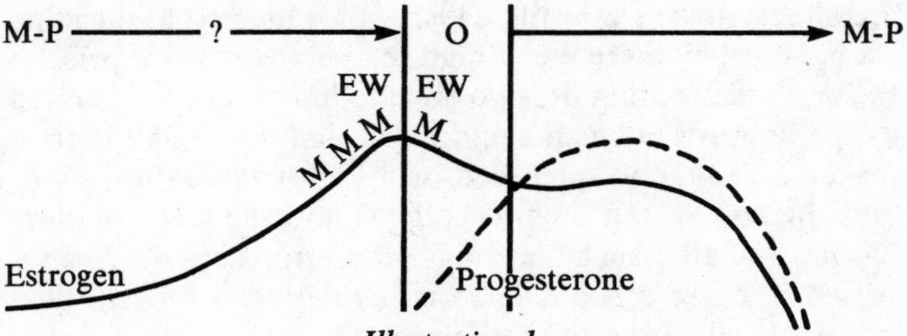

Illustration 1

A woman's cycle begins with the first day of her menstrual period. The first part of the cycle, from M-P to O, varies in length from woman to woman and from cycle to cycle in the same woman.

A feeling of wetness at the entrance of the vagina is often the first symptom of approaching ovulation. This sensation is caused by secretions reflecting a rising estrogen level.

The second part of the cycle—the interval between ovulation and the next menstruation—usually lasts twelve to sixteen days. At about the time of ovulation, progesterone causes the waking temperature to rise and to stay high until the next menstruation. The length of this high-temperature phase may vary slightly in the same woman from one month to another. It may even vary a bit more from one woman to another. It is important to remember that one woman's cycle may be quite different from that of another woman. Under special circumstances (adolescence, following childbirth, during premenopause and stress situations), the high-temperature phase may be shortened, indicating a shortened interval between ovulation and the next menstruation.

How to Evaluate the Beginning of a Cycle

The first day of a true menstrual period is the first day of the cycle (Cycle Day 1). Cycle Days 1 through 6, inclusive, are almost always infertile days. A true menstrual bleeding is one in which there was a high-temperature phase prior to the onset of bleeding. It is possible to have a cycle without a temperature rise (which could mean that no ovulation took place). Bleeding not preceded by a high-temperature phase may then occur, but such bleeding is not true menstruation. During and after such bleeding, *no* infertile days may be assumed, because it is possible that ovulation will occur during, or shortly after, the bleeding.

The probability of becoming pregnant from intercourse occurring on or before Cycle Day 6 is less than one pregnancy in 6,000 cycles. This ratio is lower than that of most methods, including the Pill. If, however, a woman has experienced cycles of 22 days or shorter, she should *not* automatically consider herself infertile through Cycle Day 6. The charts of her shortest cycles will indicate how many infertile days are likely for her during her very short cycles. Whenever more-fertile-type mucus is observed on Cycle Day 6 or earlier, it is necessary to assume fertility and to abstain from intercourse if one wishes to avoid pregnancy. If you wish to avoid pregnancy resulting from intercourse in the first phase of the cycle, you must observe two borderlines:

- In order to safely assume any infertile days beyond the Cycle Day 6 borderline, you need a good deal of experience observing your *mucus symptoms* (unless you already have a written menstrual calendar of your last 10 or more cycles and you know that your shortest cycles are 27 days or longer).

• You may apply the calculation, Shortest cycle minus 20 (S−20) as soon as you have 10 or more charted cycles. Let us assume that your shortest cycle was 27 days: 27−20=7. That means that Cycle Day 7 is the final day you may consider infertile. If you wish to go beyond the S−20 borderline, you must be particularly careful not to miss the start of the mucus. And if the mucus should happen to start before you pass the S−20 borderline, you must, of course, at once consider yourself in the fertile time.

If a true menstruation occurs and a woman is skilled in self-observation, she may be able to determine additional days beyond Cycle Day 6 to be infertile. But first she needs charting experience and, if possible, consultation with a natural-family-planning instructor.

How to Go About Self-Observation

A conception can take place only when the cervix opens up and becomes softer. The mucus becomes thin and more fluid. Sometimes there is so much of this mucus produced that it pours out like a small "waterfall" from the cervix into the vagina. This causes a condition favorable to the life of the sperm, which enables them to move quickly from the vagina, penetrate the cervical canal, and move into the uterus.

The way to go about self-observation is as follows: Every woman must go to the bathroom several times during the day. When she wipes herself, she can easily notice whether the paper glides easily over the vaginal opening as a result of any slippery, wet secretion there, or whether it tends to stick. Then she may examine the toilet tissue, to see whether mucus is visible. She can fold the paper together, unfold it,

The Cervix During Fertile and Infertile Times

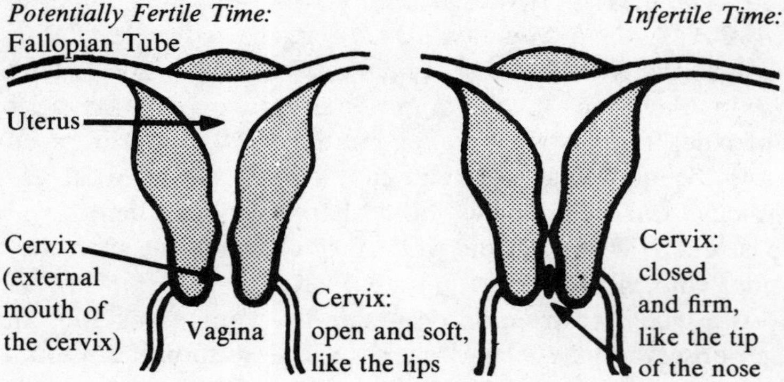

Illustration 2

and see whether the mucus is transparent or not, and to some extent stretchy, like raw egg-white (egg-white mucus: **e-w M**).

For the woman who complains of a constant vaginal discharge, in most cases, it is the stretchability of the healthy mucus that distinguishes it from this continuous discharge. The pathological discharge will usually not be stretchy. With a little practice, a woman can recognize the cervical *mucus component,* even though she may have a continual discharge.

How to Chart Your Observations

Note chart 1 (p. 20) and the symbols recorded on the middle, thick line of the chart. When your period has dwindled significantly or is over, you must decide at the end of each day:

A. Whether the day was a "dry" day. This means a real feeling of dryness at the vaginal opening, often connected with an unpleasant, itchy feeling. If so, then record a **d** on the chart for the day observed.

B. If you felt uncertain about calling it a "dry" day, and yet there was no feeling of "secreting moisture" and no visible mucus on the tissue, then record an ∅. This stands for "nothing," and we call it the interim.

C. A feeling of "secreting moisture" that was not previously observed is charted with the small letter **m.** This moisture is felt but does not appear on the tissue.

D. If you observed an increased mucus secretion, then record an **M** (for mucus) on the day observed.

- If the mucus symptom observed looks like **raw egg-white** (usually thin, clear, or cloudy, but in any case stretchy), or if it can be described as **glassy,** write **EW** or **gl** just above the **M** on your chart for that day.
- **Egg-white or glassy mucus is the typical more-fertile-type mucus.** Before and after the more-fertile-type mucus appears, another type of mucus is often observed. This other type is known as *less-fertile-type mucus.* Women have described this particular mucus as being cloudy white, milky white, or yellow (opaque); thick, lumpy, or creamy; sticky; having little or no stretchability.

Until you are skilled in self-observation, do not assume any days beyond Cycle Day 6 to be infertile.

Peak Day

The peak of an episode of mucus is the final day of more-fertile-type mucus during that episode (or the final day of *any* mucus, in an episode containing only less-fertile-type mucus).

Very important: In an episode containing more-fertile-type mucus:

- It is **the final day of more-fertile-type** mucus that is the peak of the episode. This may or may not be the day the mucus is most abundant.

• You know you are not past peak in a *mucus episode* as long as there is **any feeling of lubrication** still present. Lubrication is the slippery, wet feeling caused by the more-fertile-type mucus. This may become so thin and runny that the key to noticing it is the easy tissue glide when wiping or the awareness of slipperiness at the vaginal entrance. Understanding and paying attention to lubrication is *crucial* to correct identification of the peak day in a mucus episode.

• If the more-fertile-type mucus stops and then resumes within three days, the final day of this new appearance of more-fertile-type mucus—even if there is only one day of it—must be considered the peak. The peak of the episode is finally identified when, for three days, more-fertile-type mucus has failed to reappear.

Note: After a patch with only less-fertile-type mucus, there must be three days in a row of **d** or ∅ before marking • 1.2.3.

CHART 1

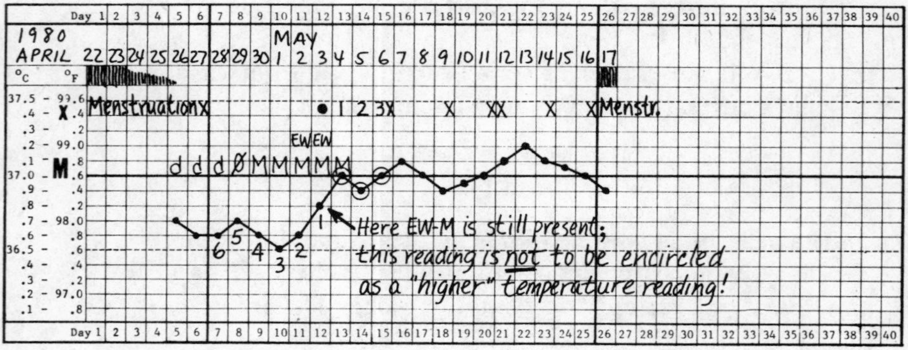

Note: Menstruation should be recorded in red, indicating the amount and duration of bleeding.

d =dry day

x =intercourse

EW =egg-white mucus

∅ =interim day (nothing felt, nothing seen)

M = mucus

• = peak day (final day of more-fertile-type mucus)

•,1,2,3 = **peak rule** (three days after a peak day are considered fertile)

Interpretation of the Chart After Childbirth (Postpartum) and During the Change of Life (Premenopause)

Chart 1 shows a single mucus episode **(M)** followed by a temperature rise—typical of the times of normal fertility during a woman's life. But after childbirth and during the change of life, long intervals without a temperature rise are more prevalent: The mucus may come and go, over and over again, *without* a temperature rise afterward. How can a postpartum or premenopausal woman know her infertile and her potentially fertile days with reliability, even in the absence of a temperature rise? She must simply pay close attention to her mucus symptom and apply the **peak rule.** Postpartum and premenopause are times of overall lower fertility in a woman's life; during these times, following the **peak rule** in the absence of a temperature rise is highly reliable. But during times of *normal* fertility, it is best, for highest reliability, to await the temperature rise after a *mucus peak* before assuming any post-peak infertility.

According to the **peak rule,** *three* days after the peak day of any episode of mucus are considered fertile. The *fourth* day after peak may, at the end of the day, be considered infertile—provided it was **d** or ∅—and so may additional days, until the mucus **(m** or **M)** begins again.

When bleeding occurs *without* a preceding high-temperature phase, the bleeding is treated as a patch of mucus (fertile), and the **final day of the bleeding is treated as the peak.** The first three days following the bleeding are considered potentially fertile—these must be three **d** or ∅ days. If mucus is present when the bleeding stops, or resumes within three days after the bleeding, then, of course, apply the **peak rule after the mucus.**

How to Take Your Waking Temperature

The most important thing to remember is to take your temperature immediately upon waking, before you get up or do any activity whatever.

Take a normal basal thermometer, already shaken down the day before, and see that it is within reach at your bedside. You do not need to take your temperature at exactly the same time every day. A difference of one and one-half hours between your earliest and latest waking times is permissible, providing all readings are taken before 7:30 A.M. (If taken later than that, the time should be recorded on the chart.) Later temperature taking will result in somewhat higher readings. If you are on a night shift and cannot take a morning waking temperature, it is important to take it at the same time every day, providing you have previously been lying down for at least one hour.

Temperature may be taken **orally, rectally,** or **vaginally. Orally,** the thermometer must be placed under the tongue and kept there from eight to ten minutes with the lips closed, breathing through the nose. **Rectal** temperatures are the most accurate. If taking your temperature **vaginally,** you must hold the thermometer.

A few days before the peak day of the cycle (or more often, within a few days afterward), the waking temperature begins to rise and stays high until shortly before menstruation. Dr. Vollman teaches his adolescent patients to take their waking temperature by explaining to them, "I want to see if your temperature makes a mountain on the chart."

Note: The completely infertile time of the cycle begins with *evening* on the 3rd day of higher temperatures after peak day. Look first for 3 readings that all lie *after* the peak and are all higher than the 6 temperatures preceding. In addition, a certain amount of rise above the preceding 6 temperatures is necessary in order to assume infertility on the 3rd such day of higher readings (*see* Appendix A).

2

After the Pill; After the I.U.D.

Mrs. V. is tired of the Pill.

"I took it, but not because I wanted to. . . ."

October 10

Dear Mrs. Trobisch,

My husband still has 3 years of school left, so we can't afford a child. When our first child does come, I don't want to have to continue working. As it is right now, we are living from my income. We really have no choice but to avoid pregnancy.

My physician, of course, prescribed the Pill. I took it, but not because I wanted to. Then I began to notice significant changes in myself. I was more irritable, gained weight easily, and lost my sexual desire. We prayed to God for help. Six days later, a friend recommended your book *The Joy of Being a Woman.*

I would like to know a little more about natural family planning.

MRS. V.

October 25

Dear Mrs. V.,

If you have any further questions about natural family planning, I suggest that you write to Dr. Roetzer.

Why don't you start right now by taking your waking temperature and observing your mucus symptoms? You can then send your charts to Dr. Roetzer, who will be able to evaluate them for you.

INGRID TROBISCH

Mrs. L. wishes to discontinue the Pill.

"My period changed; there was only a little brownish discharge . . ."

September 6

Dear Dr. Roetzer,

After taking the Pill for 6 years now, I've decided it can't go on. My period is noticeable only as a bit of brownish discharge. I hope to get a grip on this problem of family planning and to learn to master it without the Pill. I do have a few questions for you:

1. I have taken my waking temperature for three weeks without any temperature rise. Should I continue to wait, or should I see a physician?
2. Could it be that my ovaries no longer work, as a result of my having taken the Pill for so many years?
3. If a temperature shift should occur, such as you show in your book, can I consider the days afterward to be infertile, even though I've taken the Pill?

It would be a big help to both me and my husband if you could answer these questions. I'm willing to put my charts at your disposal.

MRS. L.

CHART 2

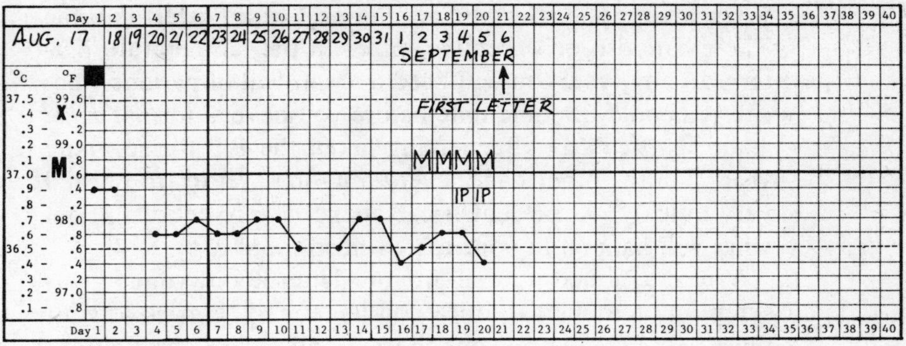

September 10

Dear Mrs. L.,

You have asked some very important questions, and it is vitally important that you have the answers to them, so I shall answer your letter at once.

After taking the Pill for such a long time, the first thing you need is patience, because you may well have to wait a long time before you observe a temperature shift. You might also experience bleeding without a preceding high-temperature phase. Such bleeding would be considered withdrawal bleeding, rather than true menstruation, and no infertile days should be assumed. The temperature might continue at a low level, or it might rise shortly after the bleeding; it is impossible to predict in advance what will happen. At this time, the most important thing is to do some careful observation and charting.

May I suggest that for the time being you make out your charts in duplicate and send me one of them as soon as you have any questions, such as how to interpret an unclear temperature rise. It is very important, after discontinuing the Pill, to have reliable temperature records. A very clear temperature shift is all that you will be able to depend upon when attempting to evaluate the onset of an infertile time. There can also be deceptive spikes in the temperature pattern. In any case, you will need a great deal of patience, because it could be some time before you have a normal cycle again, particularly after having taken the Pill for so many years. On the other hand, everything may return to normal very quickly. At present, I can make no predictions about what will happen in your case. I need more data.

You mentioned nothing in your letter about your mucus symptom, although I notice you have made entries of your *mucus observations* on your chart. Good mucus observations are the key to a more exact determination of the potentially fertile days, as well as the infertile ones. A more exact observation of your mucus symptom might be just the thing you need to get you through this time of transition.

If you have any questions whatever, don't be shy about sending your charts to me. Try to chart your mucus symptom, and on a separate sheet of paper describe, in your own words, what you've observed. Please consult with me before assuming any infertile days. A clearly interpretable chart could result, if you should notice a pronounced *mucus pattern* that is followed by three clearly elevated temperature readings. (After taking the Pill for such a long time, it would be preferable to wait for a fourth clearly elevated reading.) Once this happens, the subsequent cycles will be normal, in most cases.

DR. ROETZER

September 14

Dear Dr. Roetzer,

Thank you for the quick reply to my letter. I'll be needing your help once again, because I am still unable to interpret my temperature pattern. A temperature shift has taken place, but I'm not quite sure where the infertile days would start. I'm still having some difficulty with the mucus observation, because in years past, I never paid any attention to my mucus secretion. The days on which I entered **M** on my chart were days on which I sensed moistness at the vagina and some mucus, too, but it was more cloudy whitish in color. On the first mucus day, I noticed a cloudy white, or almost yellow, clump of mucus. It could be stretched just over an inch. I am planning to take greater care in observation of the mucus symptom. Could you possibly answer this letter within the next week or so?

MRS. L.

CHART 3

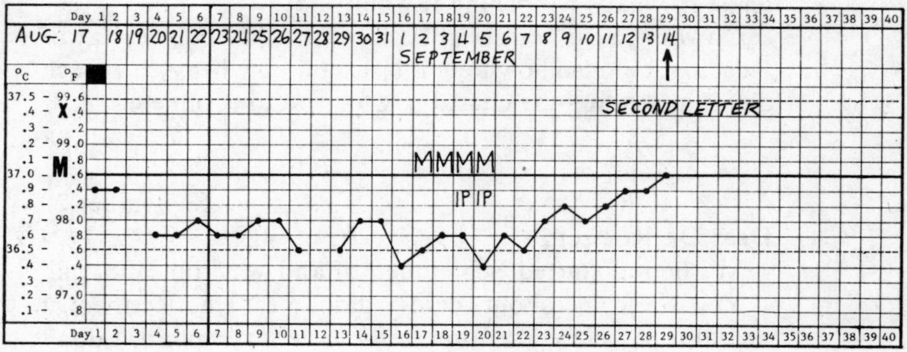

September 23

Dear Mrs. L.,

September 14 was the last day recorded on the chart that you sent to me. Things look better than I had expected, after such long use of the Pill. It is not surprising that your mucus symptom is not very pronounced, but you did do a wonderful job of describing it. An apparently genuine temperature rise began after the cessation of the mucus symptom. Your menstrual period has in the meantime almost certainly started. If you look back over this cycle, you can learn enough to evaluate the temperature rise that may occur during your next cycle. You will probably soon be able to discern infertile days following menstruation. Watch for the so-called "dry" days. Use a small **d** to chart the "dry" days occurring after menstruation.

After the "dry" days, there may be one or two days that are, for the beginner, rather nondescript, before the day on which mucus is definitely noticed.

Self-observation is a learning process that takes time, so just relax and let the various changes in sensation and appearance at the vaginal entrance show up all by themselves. You shouldn't worry about self-observation; just take an interest in what's happening in your body.

On your charts you should indicate not just the first day of bleeding, but also how long it lasts and how heavy it is each day. I'm sending the chart back for you to complete.

DR. ROETZER

September 28

Dear Dr. Roetzer,

My period started September 20 and was quite normal.

You asked me about the dry days. Yes, I notice them. I will also pay close attention to the mucus symptom. I don't know what to say about seminal fluid coming out. While I was taking the Pill, I never bothered to notice, and now we're hardly ever having intercourse—I am somewhat fearful because our second son was conceived while we were using the temperature method. Of course, at that time I knew nothing about the mucus symptom and the dry days, and nothing about the borderlines of the infertile days at the beginning of the cycle.

MRS. L.

CHART 4

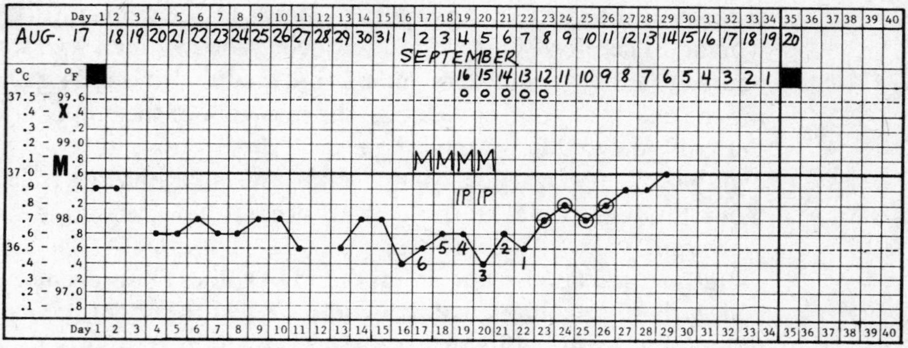

Mrs. M. tries the I.U.D.

"We've decided to have an I.U.D. inserted. . . ."

May 30

Dear Dr. Roetzer,

At first I was charting temperature and mucus observations, but then my husband and I decided to have an I.U.D. inserted anyway. At the present time we wish to avoid any chance of pregnancy, whatever the cost.

I prefer not to take the Pill, so we chose the I.U.D. Our physician said that there is a slight chance of pregnancy even with the I.U.D. in place, so I have continued to make my temperature and mucus observations as before. But I'm not sure whether these charts of my cycles since the insertion of the I.U.D. will be useful for your work.

MRS. M.

June 17

Dear Mrs. M.,

I suppose it is basically possible to continue temperature and mucus observations, even after the insertion of an

I.U.D., though you probably will notice a change in the consistency of the mucus. The experience varies from woman to woman. Therefore it is helpful to hear from women like yourself, and I would very much appreciate your sending me the charts of your cycles since the insertion of the I.U.D. Perhaps you could also send me a short description, in your own words, of the mucus symptom as you now observe it. Your findings could be quite interesting from a scientific viewpoint.

But you should also know that the I.U.D. does *not* prevent conception; it achieves its birth-control effect in an entirely different way. In reality, it mainly prevents implantation of a newly conceived human life, if conception should occur, and discharges the newly conceived life along with the next menstruation. In other words, the I.U.D. causes a very early abortion. It does not always succeed in aborting the newly conceived life, so there are, even with the I.U.D., unintended pregnancies, as you already know.

With proper observation of the waking temperature and mucus symptom, it is entirely possible to avoid conception altogether and thereby to avoid an I.U.D. induced early abortion. May I suggest that you send me your observations in about a month?

It would be unfair for me to say nothing to you about additional health hazards associated with the use of the I.U.D.: irregular bleeding, painful cramping, chronic inflammation of the endometrium, even perforation of the uterus. Women wearing the I.U.D. also experience a higher rate of tubal pregnancies, and more frequently suffer from pelvic inflammatory disease than women not wearing an I.U.D. It is also possible for the I.U.D. to come out without your noticing it. Are you aware that you should always check after any bleeding, to verify that the I.U.D. is still in place?

DR. ROETZER

August 27

Dear Dr. Roetzer,

We would like your opinion about the enclosed chart. This twenty-three-year-old woman took the Pill for four years, then had an I.U.D. inserted. Would you say that this cycle was ovulatory?

WALTER and INGRID TROBISCH

CHART 5

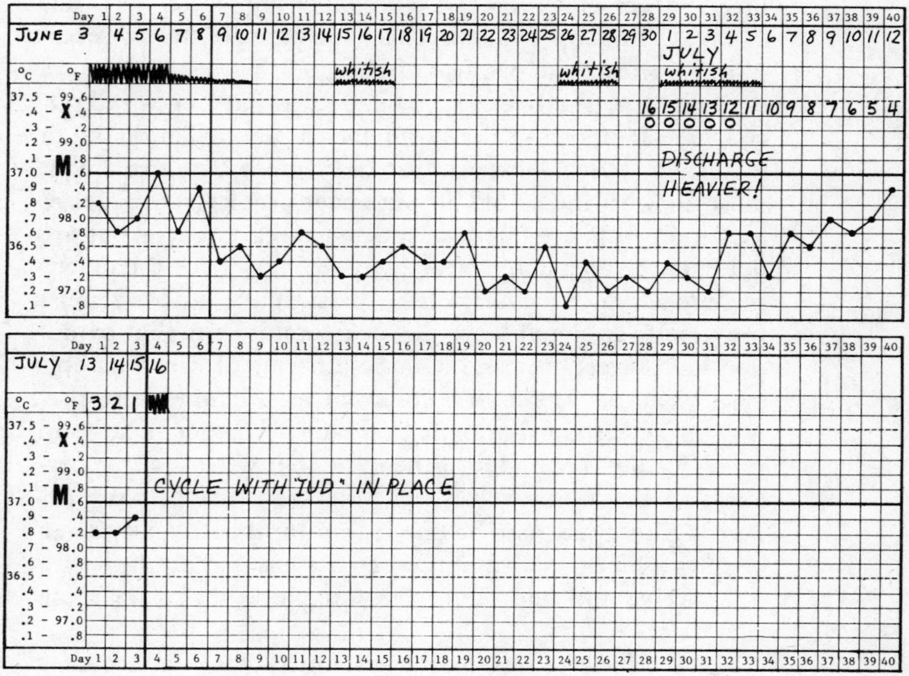

September 1

Dear Mrs. Trobisch,

In my experience, the I.U.D. disturbs the mucus and temperature signs, so that, in a few cases with which I am familiar, the temperature pattern has always been abnormal. There are a few things that can be said about this chart. The first is that this young lady did a very careful job of charting.

The 12th through 16th, last days prior to the onset of bleeding, coincide nicely with her mucus observations (I notice that three times she has charted a patch of mucus secretion that she called "whitish discharge"). These are the days one might normally expect ovulation to have occurred. Of course it is impossible to say whether or not ovulation did in fact occur. Mucus observations and temperature rise are, at most, indirect indicators of, but never proof for, the fact of ovulation. When patches of mucus secretion occur but are *not* followed by a temperature rise, we know from the mucus secretion that the ovaries have been active, and we must presume from the absence of a temperature rise that ovulation has not yet occurred. On the other hand, when an episode of mucus secretion *is* followed by a temperature rise, we can be certain that ovulation will no longer be able to occur for the remainder of the cycle, but we cannot be certain that the release of an egg from the ovary actually occurred (this appears to be one reason for the difficulty some couples with otherwise normal charts have when they wish to conceive and find themselves unable to do so for some time).

Getting back to this chart, you notice that after the days of more abundant mucus secretion, the temperature begins to climb, but only very slowly. This often happens, and is not necessarily abnormal. The least that can be said is that we do have a so-called biphasic cycle, with a low-temperature phase and a phase of sustained higher readings. I prefer to speak of a biphasic cycle, rather than an ovulatory cycle.

Evaluating the fertile and infertile days of this cycle is rather difficult. Only a few days at the beginning of the cycle may be assumed infertile. After that comes a long period of uncertainty. Not much can be said, on the basis of the rather general cervical mucus observations recorded on this chart. A temperature rise occurs just after the days of increased mucus secretion.

If we were to proceed simply on the basis of mucus observations, as does Dr. Billings, then we would have to say that there is nothing of the typical lubricative, stretchy mucus present, which Dr. Billings refers to as "fertile type mucus." If we were to assume that the days of the greatest amount of observable mucus secretion (Cycle Days 29–33) were the days of this woman's typical individual mucus, then we could say that an infertile time was present from Cycle Day 37 on. But what woman would trust herself, in such a case, to determine her infertile days solely on the basis of her mucus observation?

Perhaps you could ask this young lady a few questions:

1. Would you be willing to remove the I.U.D. to see what your normal cycle is like?

2. What was your cycle range prior to your use of the Pill or I.U.D.? (Do you have a menstrual record from which the cycle range could be computed?)

3. Do you douche?

4. Have you ever been treated for cervical erosion?

Perhaps the answers to these questions will help us to determine the reasons for the poor mucus pattern in this cycle.

I know my response has not directly answered your questions, but we need more time to investigate the matter. Perhaps the condition of her cycle will improve. Her age, her life-style (is she a student?), her daily stress, and so on, could all play a role in her cycle pattern.

DR. ROETZER

November 6

Dear Dr. Roetzer,

Mrs. Trobisch sent you my first chart, and I'm sending you the second one. Here are my answers to your questions:

1. We're now using condoms. I had the I.U.D. removed July 2.

2. I have no previous menstrual record, but I do recall that my cycles were regularly about 30 days long.

3. I don't douche; I don't use sprays, either.

4. I have never been treated for any condition of the cervix. I'm really happy that this 2nd cycle was so easy to interpret.

CHART 6

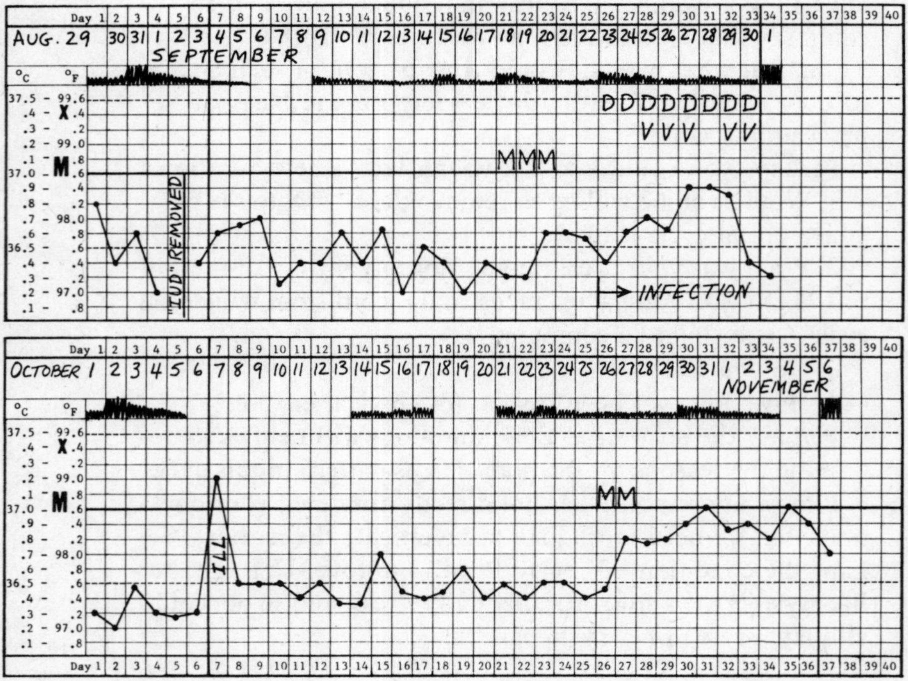

I'm charting my whitish discharge along with the same row of boxes that I use for charting my bleeding. The **D** was a white cakey discharge caused by a yeast infection, and the **V** marks when I took the medication (vaginal suppositories) prescribed for it. The **M** marks when I observed the stretchy substance, like raw egg-white. Could you help us to determine our infertile days?

MRS. O.

I'm charting my whitish discharge along the same row of boxes that I use for charting my bleeding. I have used the letter "**M**" for egg-white mucus. The whitish discharge seems to be thicker, like skin cream. **M** stands for a clear, very stretchy secretion, which can be drawn into threads. Could you help us to determine our infertile days?

MRS. O.

November 15

Dear Mrs. O.,

I agree that your previous cycle was interpretable, and I believe that, as time goes on, your cycles will get back to normal. You've done an excellent job of charting and describing your symptoms.

The essential thing to remember when evaluating the temperature curve is: Look for *"3 after peak higher than 6."* That is, look for *3* consecutive days of temperature readings, all of which lie **after peak,** and all of which are *higher* than the highest of the *six* temperature readings immediately preceding the first of those three. The completely infertile time of the cycle begins with *evening* on the day of the third such "higher" reading, *provided* the third "higher" reading reaches a certain elevation above the six preceding lower readings. (*See* Appendix A for further details.)

It is very important to notice how long the typical egg-white mucus lasts. If this egg-white mucus should still be present on the first day of elevated temperature, as was the case in your cycle, then you must wait for an additional elevated reading, so you have three of them occurring after peak day.

On your chart I have encircled the first 3 elevated readings that occur after peak day and also identified the peak day with a thick black dot. Remember that peak day is the final day showing any sign of the egg-white mucus. The completely infertile time in this cycle begins in the evening on Cycle Day 30. I don't think you'll have any trouble determining the completely infertile time in future cycles.

CHART 7

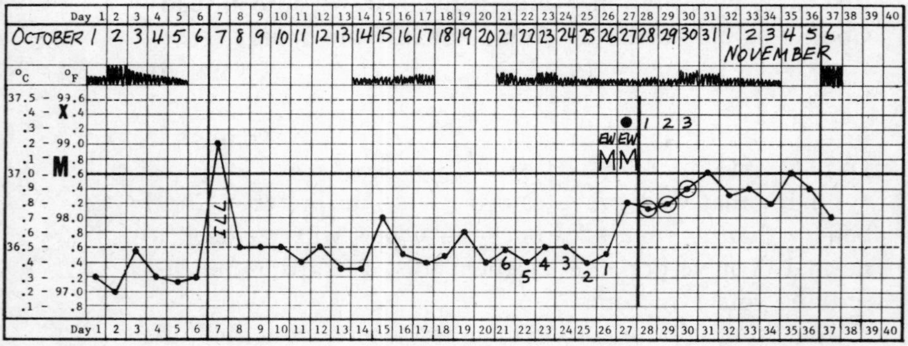

You will need patience for a while, until you are able to determine more exactly the infertile days during the first part of the cycle. A more exact observation of the mucus symptom would be a big help to you, in this regard. After your menstrual period has passed, take great care in observing your mucus symptom. Attempt first of all to distinguish what you call "whitish discharge" from cervical mucus secretion. Within the cervical mucus secretion you may notice—before and after the egg-white mucus secretion—another type of cervical mucus. It is important to be able to observe this other type of mucus prior to the appearance of the egg-white mucus, so that you can recognize the fertile days far enough in advance to avoid conceiving, if that is your wish.

I must remind you that during the mucus days, the use of contraceptive devices will not necessarily prevent pregnancy.

So have patience as you learn to master mucus observation.

DR. ROETZER

January 20

Dear Dr. Roetzer,

The information you have given me has been extremely helpful. During these two cycles, it was easy for me to mark the six low temperatures and the following high ones. My periods are fairly light and short now, which I appreciate, and I am able to detect the stretchy mucus (egg-white mucus) easily.

In the first cycle, on the 17th and 19th days, where I have marked a capital **W**, there was a great deal of wetness—like water—but no whitish discharge or stretchy mucus. In the second cycle, on the 27th day I felt a sharp pain on my lower left side. I wondered if that might be the so-called intermenstrual pain. On the 24th day of that cycle, I took my temperature late in the day (11:00 A.M.) which is why it is high (usually I take my temperature between 6:00 and 6:30A.M., vaginally). I have encircled four higher readings in the bottom chart because egg-white mucus was still present on the first day of high temperature.

I'm glad I got in touch with you. I feel much better physically since I stopped the Pill and I.U.D. Besides that, it's fascinating to be able to observe and understand how my body functions.

MRS. O.

CHART 8

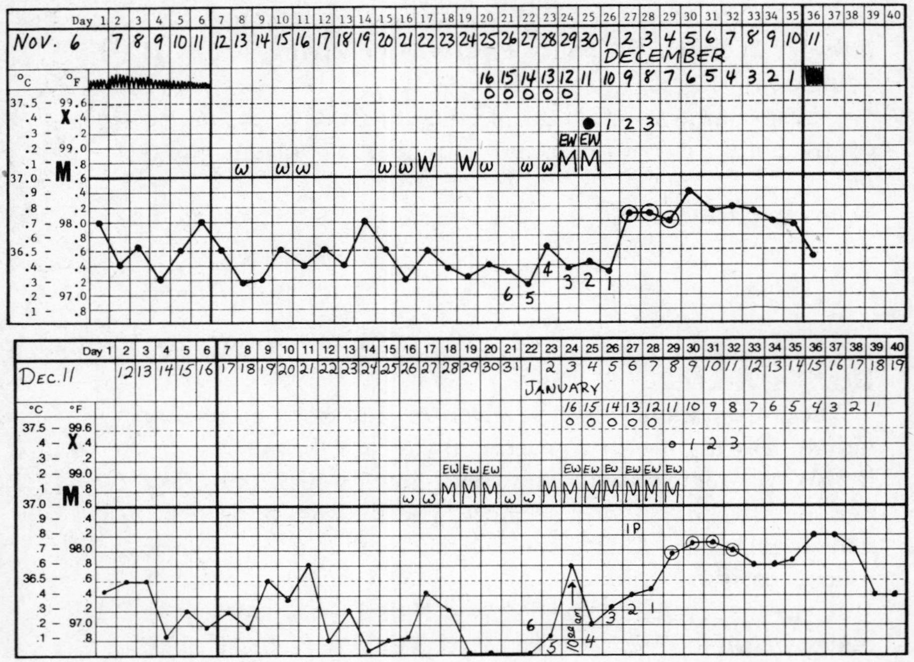

Note: The small **w** on this chart is this woman's symbol for "whitish discharge: thicker, like skin cream." It is the usual procedure to encircle only those elevated readings which lie after peak; this woman proceeded correctly, however, in that she knew she needed to have *three* elevated readings, all *after* the peak, in order to assume complete infertility for the remainder of the cycle.

3

The Myth of Multiple Ovulation

February 6

Dear Mrs. Trobisch,

I completely agree with everything you said about pregnancy, birth, and breast-feeding, and I would like to emphasize that I have personally experienced it all. I think what you said about the value of breast-feeding and the manner in which it should be done is really important. I hope with all my heart that your suggestions win a wide hearing.

But—and this is my big question—is the sympto-thermal method reliable? Right now, I'm thinking of friends and relatives. They were so enthusiastic about your book and depended on their waking-temperature pattern to avoid conceiving, but got pregnant anyway. In the cases I'm thinking of, the mothers were already overtaxed, physically and emotionally, by their other children. I consider these surprise pregnancies something of a tragedy for that reason alone, completely apart from considerations of living space and finances. It's my personal opinion that these children are not viewed by God as "accidents," but I still must question the reliability of the sympto-thermal method.

You wrote in your book, "The change in the temperature

is due to the secretion of the hormone progesterone, which also prevents the release of another ovum from the ovary. It is important to remember this, because it means that in each cycle there is an *unmistakable* definite phase of infertility that can be recognized from the rise in temperature." And on page 49, "The combination of the observation of the cervical mucus which helps to recognize in advance the approach of ovulation, plus the observation of the temperature rise, offers the highest possible certainty of determining fertility and infertility."

I must object to this. My husband and I observed my waking temperature and recommended the temperature method to other couples *until* about eight or ten years ago. We read in a magazine that, according to medical science, there can easily be several ovulations during a single cycle. I also spoke with my gynecologist a short time ago and asked him about the sympto-thermal method. "The method only works," he told me, "for those women who are, so to speak, sterile anyway—at least that's my experience." He also confirmed that an ovulation can be triggered at any time by excitement, fear, a change in the weather, and so on. So you really can't give the sympto-thermal method a 0.7% failure rate, as you did on page 55 of your book.

Mrs. Trobisch, this problem has been keeping me awake nights. Do you think those disappointed couples will take to heart the beautiful things you say about delivery and breast-feeding once they've trusted what you had to say about avoiding pregnancy and became unwilling parents? I can still hear one bitter remark: "Make sure you don't recommend *that* book to anyone else again." I just don't know what can be done, now that the book has been printed and is in the stores. Perhaps you could insert a short correction notice in the unsold books. Precisely because you wrote the book as a Christian, every part of it should be credible and sound.

I know you'll not be angry with me because I've spoken openly; I really felt that I had to say what I've said.

With best wishes,
MRS. K.

February 21

Dear Mrs. K.,

Because your letter to Mrs. Trobisch pertained exclusively to medical matters touched upon in *The Joy of Being a Woman,* I have suggested to her that I reply.

I understand, of course, that given the present bias in public opinion, the kind of conception regulation described by Mrs. Trobisch will be met with skepticism. Even in medical schools, the curriculum contains too little about the physiology of the menstrual cycle; I know only too well the negative attitude prevalent among practicing gynecologists toward natural family planning. I must simply point out to all these ladies and gentlemen that they make rash judgments because they have not studied the relevant material pertaining to this medical specialty. Worst of all, sincere couples seeking advice and relying upon the expertise of their physicians are left needlessly confused.

Now, regarding your question about the second or third ovulation or about the ovulation that might simply occur "at any time" because of "excitement, fear, a change in the weather, and so on." There isn't a single documented case, in all medical literature, proving that an additional ovulation occurred or might have occurred from these causes, once the high-temperature plateau reflecting the activity of the corpus luteum has been reached. On the contrary, there are charts from hundreds of thousands of cycles indicating that after the high-temperature plateau is reached, a completely infertile time of the cycle is present.

You might wonder how I can be so certain of my answer, and you deserve a reply. First of all, I am familiar with the most important medical studies published in German, English, and French, and I have copies of them all in my personal library. In addition, I have spent almost thirty years—since spring of 1951—investigating the matter intensively. International foundations have invited me to their symposia, and the World Health Organization asked me to come to a meeting of experts in Geneva in February 1976.

At these international symposia, whether in Washington, D.C. (June 1973), or in Rome (April 1974), in Boston (May 1975), or in Geneva (February 1976), New York (1978), or Washington, D.C. (1979), there were always a dozen or so persons from every corner of the globe who had either studied the matter theoretically or tested it in practice. Among them were research scientists who were somewhat reserved about the practical applicability of the knowledge we had at our disposal. But there was one thing that all the experts were agreed upon: There is a narrowly defined and identifiable infertile phase of the cycle, and it is certain that there is no second ovulation during the luteal phase.

Those who attempted to assert the presence of such second ovulations were severely criticized. It is because of these old wives' tales—without any solid reference to fact, yet repeated over and over again for the last 100 years—that confusion and insecurity continue to be generated. Among the experts, and not least in the opinion of the World Health Organization, no one could deny that there is no proof in the entire medical literature of the world that a second ovulation or a conception ever occurred during the pronounced luteal phase.

Mrs. Trobisch is quite correct in the claims she makes about the reliability of the natural-family-planning method she describes, and there is no reason for her to include a correction notice, as if there were something to retract in what she said.

In addition to defending the claims Mrs. Trobisch made, may I also offer a few constructive suggestions?

Please ask the physician who told you the story about second ovulations to send me proof of such a fact—either primary data or references to the literature. Otherwise, he should not pass on such unfounded rumors.

If anyone claims to have had an unexpected pregnancy, I suggest that the chart for that cycle be sent to me, together with the charts for the previous cycle. The chart should at least show where the temperature rise is located (where the first 3 readings higher than the immediately preceding 6 lower readings are to be found) and when genital contact occurred during this time span. In some cases, the observation of cervical mucus is even more important, but not every woman is immediately able to make such observations. Making observations and charting are part of a gradual learning process, but in time they become second nature.

At present, I am doing research under contract with an American foundation and am gathering data from thousands of cycles like the one illustrated on the sample chart that I have enclosed with this letter. This young woman, born in 1947, has two children and is making complete observations. I make comments on each client's charts and send them back to her. And I pursue each case of pregnancy very carefully, because the couple concerned can learn a great deal from an evaluation of the cycle in which conception occurred. The number of unexpected pregnancies stands at less than one per 100 women-years of use, as mentioned by Mrs. Trobisch in her book *The Joy of Being a Woman.* Every similar investigation in which couples have received careful follow-up and counseling reports the same degree of reliability. There has never been a pregnancy from intercourse occurring after the third day of encircled "higher" readings, provided that certain basic conditions are met: No reading may be encircled unless it occurs after the cessation of more-fertile-type mucus secretion, and the third encircled reading must be at least .36° F. (.2° C.) higher than the highest of the final six lower readings.

CHART 9

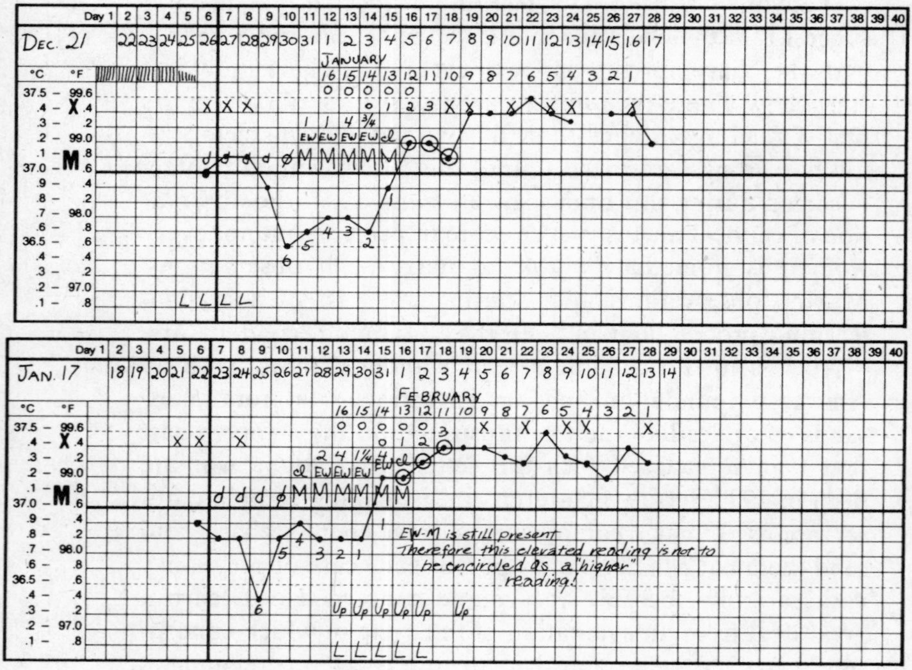

Note: cl M — Mucus that is cloudy white (may also be somewhat sticky). Less-fertile-type mucus
Up — Up frequently during the night
L — Unusually late to bed the night before
Up and **L** can lead to an artificial rise in temperature.

It is a pleasure for me to note how very willing many women are to cooperate, once they have discovered for themselves the value in self-observation of the cervical mucus secretion. And it is also surprising how often women with irregular cycles find their cycles becoming more regular as they learn to follow the course of their cycles and lose their anxiety about where they stand in the cycle.

I would also be happy to have you refer any woman to me who claims to have had an unintended pregnancy. I have developed a correspondence course, and I can send the necessary instructions in proper sequence. It is insufficient to simply read the instruction sheet that comes with a basal thermometer or to attempt to practice family planning solely on the basis of what is contained in a short introductory essay designed to interest couples, rather than to instruct them adequately. In my own instructions, I try to impress upon clients that they should first make their own observations and *ask me plenty of questions* before attempting to determine for themselves the fertile and infertile days of the cycle. If a competent counselor is available, it may be possible to interpret the very first cycle of observation and charting. In fact, I myself offer immediate evaluation and advice by telephone for those who desire such a service.

"The future," a German professor of gynecology once said, "belongs to natural family planning." If numerous couples would simply cooperate in providing data, we could very quickly convince skeptics of the truth of that statement. The very least we could do at the present time would be to demonstrate that the sympto-thermal method, correctly understood and followed, is just as effective for the purpose of avoiding pregnancy as taking the Pill, but without damage to a woman's health.

With cordial best wishes I remain,

Sincerely yours,
DR. ROETZER

February 26

Dear Dr. Roetzer,

Thank you very much for the detailed reply to my previous letter. I found it really interesting. As I said in my letter to Mrs. Trobisch, my husband and I are thoroughly familiar with the sympto-thermal method and are successful users. And I completely agree with Mrs. Trobisch when she says on page 61, ". . . Natural Family Planning is not simply an approach to contraception with greater advantages or disadvantages. It actually offers a new way of life, because it is based on a different image of man." I can honestly say that it frightens me to think of my own daughter taking the Pill for years, or even decades! And there is no doubt in my mind that the level of public morality would be higher today, were it not for the invention of the Pill, with all the social consequences that go with its promotion and use.

I don't know whether it will be possible for me to convince my friend with the unintended pregnancy to learn more about your method. Nor am I certain I'll be able to contact the gynecologist I mentioned in my letter. I did have the opportunity to speak with him in detail about second ovulations during a lengthy stay at the hospital during a recent illness. But perhaps I can come back to that matter at a later time and send you the information you requested, if and when I should receive any. In any case, I just wanted to answer your letter and express my gratitude to you.

You mentioned that you have developed a correspondence course. I found the following comments of yours particularly informative: "It is insufficient to simply read the instruction sheet that comes with a basal thermometer, or to attempt to practice natural family planning solely on the basis of what is contained in a short introductory essay designed to interest couples, rather than to instruct them adequately. In my own instructions, I try to impress upon my clients that they should first make their own observations and ask plenty of questions." Don't you think it would have been a good idea to put such a warning in chapter 3 of Mrs. Trobisch's book? After looking through the material you sent to me, I tend to believe that our real concern is not so much with second ovulation as with more comprehensive schooling in natural family planning.

And again, thank you so much for your concern and the detailed letter. It was really very helpful.

MRS. K.

Stress and the Cycle Pattern

Mrs. N. is the mother of 3 children and has been a participant in a course on the sympto-thermal method. Her previous cycle range is 28 to 30 days. This cycle is completely different:

CHART 10

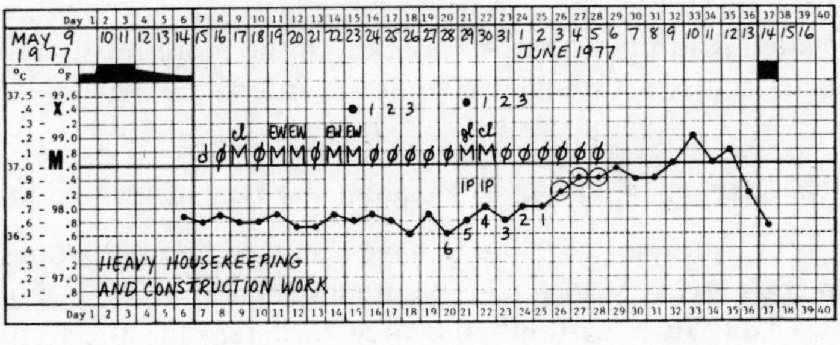

Mrs. N. knew that stress (see notation on her chart, "Heavy housekeeping and construction work") could cause a prolongation of the early part of the cycle, so she paid careful attention to the mucus symptom and waited for her temperature rise. When three interim days followed Day 15 (May 23), she designated Day 15 as the peak day of that first episode of mucus, once she saw that the **e-w M** present through Day 15 had failed to return during the three days afterward. She also noticed that the temperature did not begin to rise following the first episode of mucus; she expected mucus might return before an eventual temperature rise. When on Day 21 glassy mucus appeared, she realized that this single day of glassy mucus might prove to be the peak day of the cycle. She waited for her temperature to rise. By Day 25, she was able to place the large dot and the 1,2,3 on Days 21–24. Beginning with Day 26, she was able to begin to encircle the three consecutive readings all lying *after* the second peak and all higher than the immediately preceding six temperatures.

Prolongations of the early phase of the cycle (or, to be more exact, delay of the ovulatory phase) may be occasioned by illness, travel, or traumatic experiences occurring during this time. The important thing is to wait for the three elevated readings *after* the cessation of the more-fertile-type mucus before assuming a completely infertile time.

The Danger of Trying to Pinpoint the Day of Ovulation

A few surprise pregnancies have occurred because women (or their gynecologists) have attempted to pinpoint some exact "day of ovulation" and then to determine the fertile and infertile days accordingly. The following example illustrates this mistake. Mrs. T. has 3 children, and she begins her charting on the basis of what she has read in *The Joy of Being a Woman.* She writes the following:

Dear Mrs. Trobisch,

From the very first month I charted, I was able to tell exactly when ovulation occurred, because I felt the intermenstrual pain and saw the mucus. I took my temperature very carefully. But now I'm pregnant! On this chart, you can see without any doubt that ovulation occurred on Cycle Day 14—and we didn't have intercourse until Cycle Day 18. I've completely lost faith in this method.

MRS. T.

CHART 11

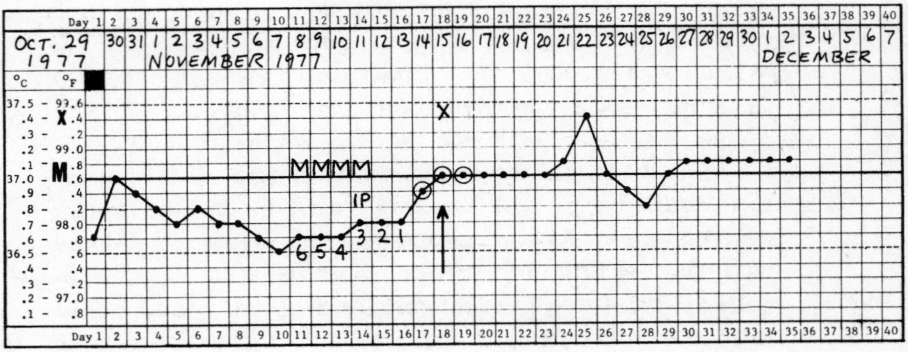

Dear Mrs. T.,

It is not possible to pinpoint a "day of ovulation." Rather one must learn to determine the beginning and the end of the potentially fertile time. The most important rule to remember is this: The completely infertile time of the final phase of the cycle begins with evening on the third day of those high-temperature readings that occur after cessation of the more-fertile-type mucus. The third encircled reading must be at least .36° F. (.2° C.) above the highest of the preceding six low readings (here numbered in reverse).

It is a shame that printed temperature graphs are still being sold with misleading sample charts that designate the lowest point in the temperature pattern as the day of ovulation. Apart from the fact that only a small fraction of all temperature curves show an unmistakable low point, it is totally incorrect to assume that ovulation must have occurred at the low point. Neither do intermenstrual pain or the final day of egg-white mucus (the peak day) directly indicate the precise time of ovulation.

DR. ROETZER

Dear Mrs. Trobisch,

My husband and I read *The Joy of Being a Woman* and decided to follow the sympto-thermal method of family planning described in that book. I stopped taking the Pill. When I was taking the Pill, I missed the changing moods of the natural cycle, I worried about side effects, and I felt very much alone, as I swallowed the Pill each day.

My husband did the actual charting, and we found ourselves quite happy with this cooperative method of conception regulation. As you can see from our charts, we did very well with the little information available to us.

I later went to a gynecologist for a physical, and I naturally took my charts with me. He was at first skeptical, then grew more interested as he looked at them. It was his opinion that I had been assuming too many fertile days, and he made the corrections on my chart that are written in.

CHART 12

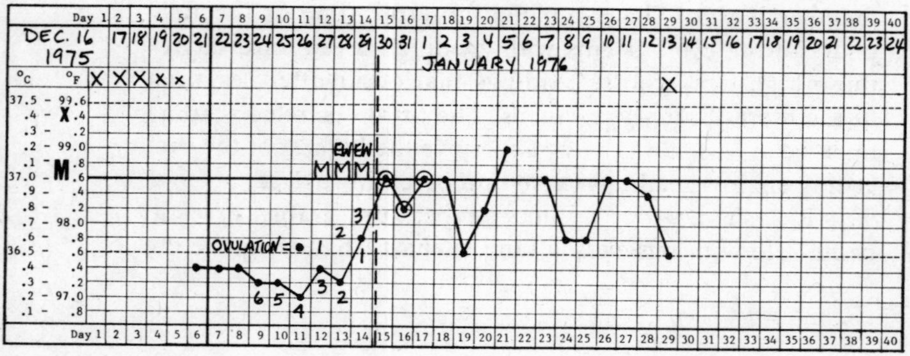

According to him, the very lowest temperature (indicated by the large dot in cycles number 4 and 5) was the day of ovulation, and three days later was the end of the fertile time. We were really irritated, because my doctor's evaluation scarcely corresponded with my own.

That was cycle number 4. Now look at cycle number 5. My confidence shaken, I made a mish-mash out of my charting—even of the mucus symptom—with the result that our daughter was born October 19, 1976. We are naturally very happy about our baby, but our trust and our joy in using the sympto-thermal method were very much damaged.

CHART 13

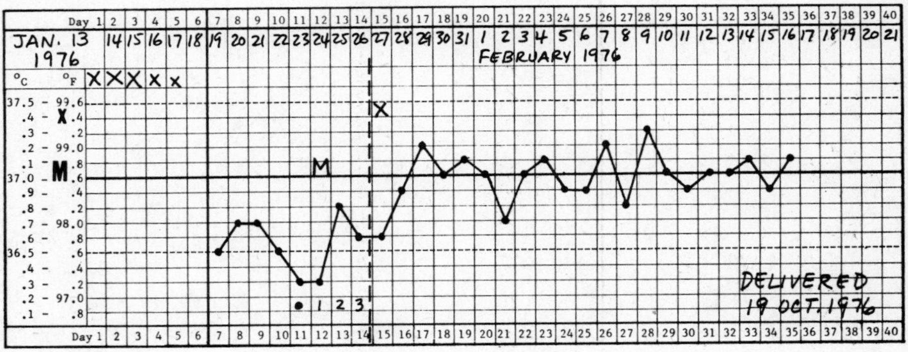

Note: The completely infertile time begins with evening on the third day of "higher" readings—Cycle Day 18 on this chart.

After this pregnancy—that is, after the first menstrual period following delivery—I took the Pill again, but only for about a month. Cramps appeared, and pain in my legs. So we tried your method again. Evaluating the cycle was too much for me; besides, there was a long period of abstinence, and my gynecologist was warning me against "experiments" (as he called them). I panicked and took the Pill again—this time for six months.

Not long afterward, hoping against hope, we tried a third time, and this time followed the rules of the sympto-thermal method exactly (my husband usually suggested that we add an extra day, just to be safe). If I'm uncertain about the evaluation of the cycle, we simply abstain a little longer.

My gynecologist was upset when I told him that I wasn't going to take the Pill anymore and that we were going to follow the sympto-thermal method. We had a big argument, which he concluded by saying, "I'll laugh all the way home, when you come back next month pregnant!" Well, it's been seven months now, and we're the ones who are laughing.

MRS. V.

4

A Gradual Learning Process

Miss J. was nineteen years old and unmarried.

"At first it was a bother. . . ."

August 21

Dear Dr. Roetzer,

I found your book fascinating and read it carefully from cover to cover. Then I started taking my temperature. At first it was a bother, but I got used to it, and now it's second nature. In fact I really enjoy taking my temperature now, and plan to continue it in the future.

But I do have one question. I'd like to know when the fertile time begins for me and, above all, when ovulation occurs. I've enclosed copies of my charts, and as you can see, I am able to detect mucus very seldom and often not at all. I would like your opinion on my charting and what I could do to improve it.

MISS J.

CHART 14

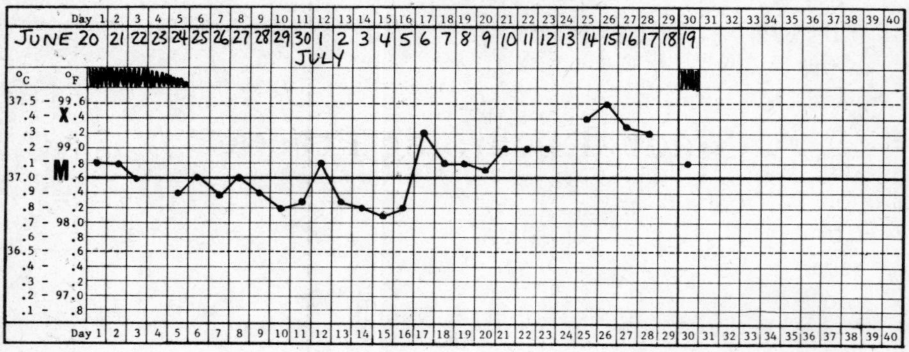

September 3

Dear Miss J.,

It is a very common experience for women to find that they quickly get accustomed to taking their waking temperature. Initial difficulties, such as you yourself experienced, must of course be overcome. The more closely you learn to observe the mucus symptom, the better able you will be to determine your potentially fertile days. It is not important to pinpoint the day of ovulation; it's not even possible to do so. The important thing is to be able to answer the question "When do my potentially fertile days begin, and when do they end?"

I'm sure you'll understand how important a more exact observation of the mucus symptom can be. Experience shows that almost every woman is able to notice the mucus symptom. If you have not yet noticed it, it could be that you have simply never attributed any particular significance to it and have therefore not paid much attention to it.

Ovulation need not occur at the same time in each cycle. It might occur earlier than usual. But if you have learned to observe your mucus symptom and are able to notice the presence of cervical mucus for a period of several days, you will be alerted well in advance of the approaching ovulation. If the ovulation is about to occur earlier than usual in the cycle, the cervical mucus will also appear earlier than usual. Try to observe and chart your mucus symptom daily, beginning the day after your period is finished. This self-observation is a gradual learning process. A forced, or strained, self-observation is not at all necessary. With time, you will become increasingly aware of the differences in sensation and what you see.

After you have charted a cycle while attempting this more careful observation of mucus symptom, please send the chart to me for review. During the first cycle of observation, you would do well to include an additional sheet of paper on which you write down, in your own words, your daily observations. Later on, abbreviated symbols on the chart will be sufficient.

If you still find yourself unable to observe cervical mucus secretion, please let me know. There is another method by which you may be able to detect the cervical mucus symptom.

DR. ROETZER

October 16

Dear Dr. Roetzer,

You were right. By paying closer attention to my mucus symptom, I was able to easily detect it during this cycle. I found that the mucus would stretch almost an inch, but that was only on one day. On the following days, I had only a moist sensation at the vulva, and although I could see the mucus, it was no longer stretchable.

Is it correct to assume that as long as the mucus is present, ovulation has not yet occurred? Thank you very much for any help you can give me in this matter.

MISS J.

CHART 15

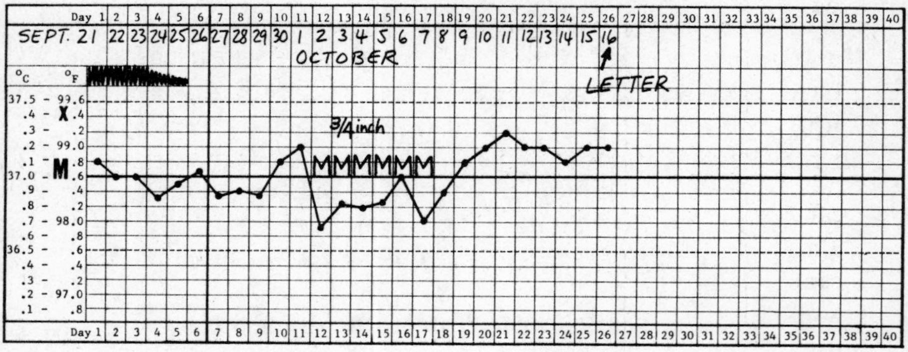

Dear Miss J.,

You have done a nice job with your observations during the cycle beginning September 21. To prevent any misunderstanding, you should write down **E-W** over the **M** on your chart, to indicate the so-called egg-white mucus—the stretchy kind of mucus you mentioned. Some women prefer to describe it as glassy mucus (it can also be a crystal-clear, stretchy mucus). Which expression do you prefer?

Until you are able to distinguish without difficulty your egg-white mucus from other kinds, you should assume that all days on which mucus is observed are still pre-ovulation. However, with practice, it should be possible to easily distinguish the days of egg-white mucus from others. This should give you enough information to evaluate all the days of your cycle. Please take into consideration that sometimes a woman cannot see stretchy mucus but still may have the feeling of wetness, together with a lubricative sensation. As long as this sensation is present, more-fertile-type-mucus has not as yet ended. The last day of lubrication is peak day. If this is the case, please write *slippery* or *lubricative* in the columns of each of the days on which the sensation was noticed.

DR. ROETZER

Mrs. D., recently married, fears further pregnancy.

"I'm not very satisfied with this method. . . ."

June 26

Dear Dr. Roetzer,

I'm not very satisfied with this method. We married only recently and do not wish to restrict our lovemaking to just a few days each cycle. As it is, we generally have relations during the first seven days of the cycle, and thereafter (but not very often) use withdrawal. But even that is not very satisfying, since we fear having a child. Because of the strain this is placing on our marriage, I have almost decided to take the Pill.

Can you give us any advice?

MRS. D.

CHART 16

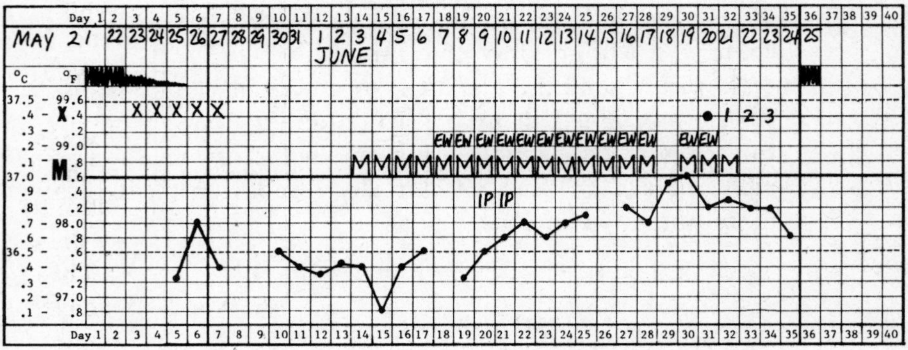

June 30

Dear Mrs. D.,

Thank you for your frank comments. I am, of course, quite willing to help you determine more exactly your potentially fertile days. The first thing you need to do is improve your observation of the mucus symptom, in order to evaluate your cycle more easily. I notice that you observed mucus from Cycle Day 14 through Cycle Day 32 and indicated it as egg-white mucus from Cycle Day 18 onward. There remain only 4 days after peak day—as you have evaluated it—until the onset of menses. The temperature pattern is clearly biphasic, having first a low and then a high phase. And it was quite correct of you not to encircle any of the high readings. One of the most important rules is that no high readings may be encircled unless they occur *after* the egg-white mucus has ceased.

Now I have a question for you: Was all of the mucus that you charted as egg-white mucus stretchy, elastic, stringy, glassy, transparent? Would you describe for me, in your own words, what you have indicated on your chart as egg-white mucus?

Some women have a continuous discharge, but are nevertheless able, after a while, to distinguish their discharge from the cervical mucus symptom. The most important difference is that the continuous discharge is usually not stretchy; it will not draw into threads.

So please send me a short note describing, in your own words, your mucus symptom. I would then like to send you further instructions, depending on whether or not the egg-white mucus on your chart really stands for the typical more-fertile-type mucus.

DR. ROETZER

July 28

Dear Dr. Roetzer,

The **E-W M** entries on the chart I sent you were based on a misunderstanding on my part. I had imagined egg-white mucus to refer to an opaque white discharge, like the white of a hard-boiled egg. I definitely prefer the term *glassy;* it fits better.

I would describe my mucus symptom as follows: Glassy mucus is easy to stretch, and clear. Afterwards, I notice a whitish, lumpy, sticky mucus. I have redrawn my previous chart beginning May 21 and included with it the cycle beginning on June 25. I have tried to follow the advice given in your guidelines. Would you say that I could now rely securely on my own evaluation of the fertile and infertile days?

MRS. D.

CHART 17

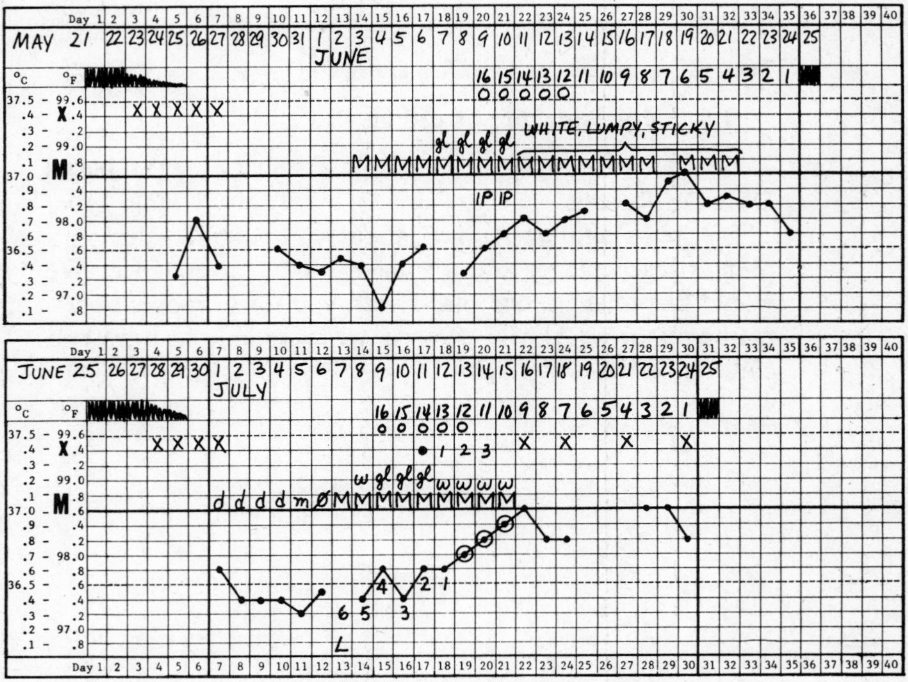

Note: The small **w** on this chart represents the "whitish, lumpy, sticky" mucus described by Mrs. D.

August 4

Dear Mrs. D.,

Yes, you have correctly interpreted your charts. You have indicated as peak day the final day of any sign of glassy mucus. And the subsequent days of white, lumpy, and sticky mucus are rightly judged to be post-peak days.

The reverse numeration from 1–16 beginning from the final day of the cycle indicates that your observation of the mucus symptom nicely coincided with the potential days of ovulation (the last 12 through 16 days).

You will certainly be successful in evaluating your future cycles if you continue such excellent observation and charting.

DR. ROETZER

Mrs. P., housewife, shares her charts.

"I found greater inner freedom. . . ."

October 8

Dear Dr. Roetzer,

Ten years ago we learned about your method during a premarriage course, and we have used it ever since. We would like to share our charts with you for purposes of scientific research. As you can see, we were able to have two children at the desired time.

MRS. P.

CHART 18

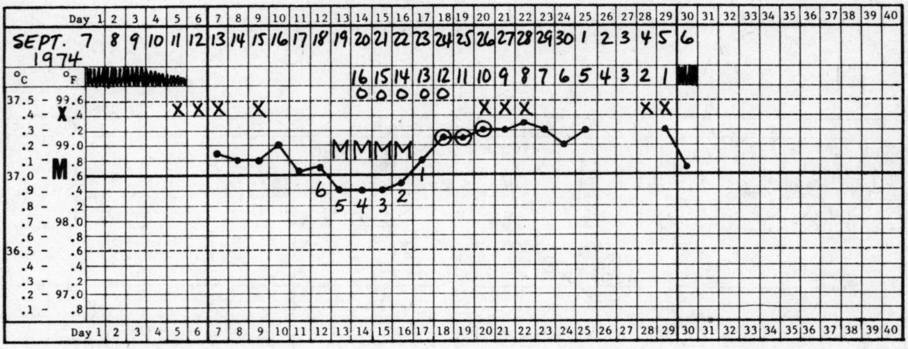

October 20

Dear Mrs. P.,

You have done an excellent job of charting and were rightly confident in your evaluation of each cycle.

In recent years, further developments have taken place in the field of natural family planning, particularly with respect to self-observation of the mucus symptom.

I would very much like to hear what you have to say about this more exact observation of the mucus symptom.

DR. ROETZER

December 4

Dear Dr. Roetzer,

Thank you very much for the helpful instructions that you sent to me. I did attempt to discern differences within the cervical mucus symptom during my last cycle, and I hope to pass on to my friends what I have just learned. It is really possible to determine one's mucus symptom by sensation and by using tissue paper. I have also discovered something very helpful for accurate mucus observation. The cheaper, plain, less-absorbent tissue helps you to get a better reading of the mucus than does the higher-quality, soft tissue.

CHART 19

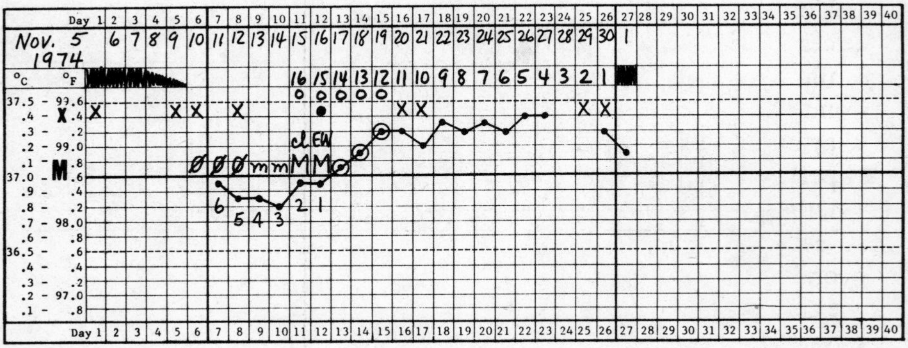

Note: On Cycle Days 9 and 10, this woman experienced a feeling of secreting moisture at the opening of the vagina—a feeling that previously was not present. There was nothing at all on the tissue. Therefore, only the small letter **m** is charted, for moistness. It could be that this sensation, when regularly occurring before **M** appears on the tissue, would indicate that all days prior to this sensation are infertile. That is true for the woman who delivered the above chart. In the meantime, this couple tried to achieve a third pregnancy and was successful. Now they are again using natural family planning.

As I look back over ten years of marriage, I have much to thank you for, Dr. Roetzer. Because of your efforts in natural family planning, I have found greater inner freedom and self-direction.

MRS. P.

December 15

Dear Mrs. P.,

Your attempts to differentiate the various traits in the mucus symptom throughout the cycle are outstanding.

You mentioned that you intend to pass on your experiences to your friends. May I caution them to remember that, while learning, a woman should not assume infertility beyond the first six days of the cycle. They should do careful charting and observation, and only after they are thoroughly experienced—like yourself—will it be possible to say whether additional days beyond the first six days may safely be assumed infertile. I am, of course, quite willing to correspond with your friends, to help them determine whether they may safely assume infertile days beyond the first six days.

DR. ROETZER

Testimonies:

A mother of three children

It was by the grace of God that I discovered your method from Mrs. N. just two years ago. I feel that our marriage has since become richer and deeper. I changed physicians because mine told me that I was crazy to try your method, but the new one has accepted it as "the only right and beautiful way" of family planning.

A mother of six children

I had a lot of anxiety when I first began making temperature and mucus observations, but I don't even give it a second thought anymore. I have come to observe myself just as I do the changes in the weather and the growth of plants about the house.

A mother of two children

I am very thankful that I was privileged to find such a wonderful method of conception regulation.

Miss E., student, wishes to marry, but wants to avoid pregnancy until after her studies are completed.

"We can't stand the abstinence. . . ."

March 5

Dear Dr. Roetzer,

Four months ago, as a result of my contacts with the Trobisch family, I began to chart my waking temperature very carefully. I've enclosed copies of these charts and hope that you will be able to help me with the determination of my fertile and infertile days. I'm sorry to say that I haven't paid much attention to my mucus symptom so far, but I hope to observe it more carefully in the future, according to whatever instructions I get from you. I am engaged and plan to get married next summer. My fiancé and I wish to be well prepared. Both of us are still in college and would like to postpone having a family until our studies are completed.

It makes me happy to think that God has given us natural ways for responsible planning of our families. I rejoice that He has used you as His instrument for making these natural ways available to all.

I do have one problem. I come from a large family, and my mother, in particular, has been pestering me to take the Pill. She says the temperature method is not safe and we'll never be able to endure the tensions of abstinence, particularly during the early part of our marriage. One of my sisters is now being treated by a gynecologist who told her not to try natural methods because their failure rate is too high. You can understand why I'm beginning to lose confidence in the method of natural family planning so simply portrayed by Ingrid Trobisch in her book. Besides that, I have noticed that the various bodily signs don't coincide for me:

I don't seem to have intermenstrual pain, my temperature does not always return to a low level by the time my period starts, and my mucus secretion shows different aspects.

So, please help me. Which method do you think will work best for me? I've spoken with my fiancé about this matter frequently.

Thanking you in advance for your response, which I await impatiently.

MISS E.

CHART 20

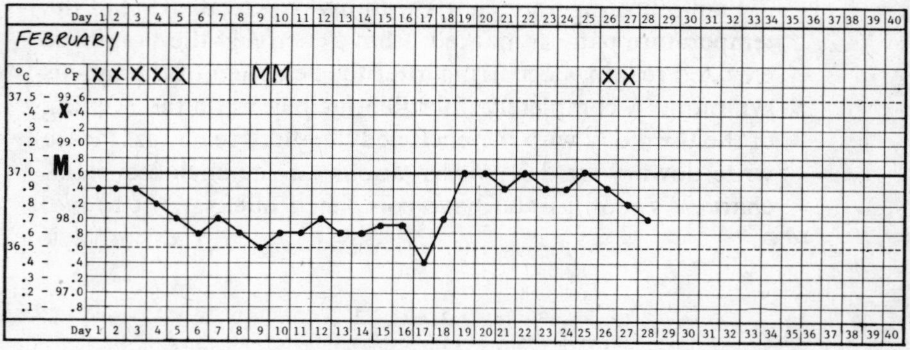

March 25

Dear Miss E.,

Thank you for your very frank letter. I can well appreciate how easy it is for you to become confused and uncertain, when you are told from all sides that temperature and mucus observation are not trustworthy. The matter of abstinence is, of course, something that you two, as an engaged couple, must earnestly discuss in order to come to a mutual understanding.

The amount of abstinence required is dependent on the kind of observations that are made. I can assure you that there are some young couples with temperature patterns requiring more abstinence than will apparently be necessary in your case. In spite of this, together they have mastered the task of abstinence.

You've done some very nice charting, and it can be interpreted without great difficulty. The interpretation would be easier for you if you could improve the quality of your observations of the mucus symptom. Self-observation of the mucus symptom is something that will become self-evident with time and patience, without forcing or straining yourself. This is a gradual learning process, so be patient. Intermenstrual pain is not so very important, and besides, many women under thirty do not notice it at all.

I am returning your charts with my own evaluation of the temperature pattern marked. I have encircled the first three elevated readings occurring after the cessation of the mucus symptom. A completely infertile time begins on the evening of the third day with the encircled "higher" readings. Please write down your daily observations on the enclosed blank charts. As soon as you have completed one, send it to me.

DR. ROETZER

CHART 21

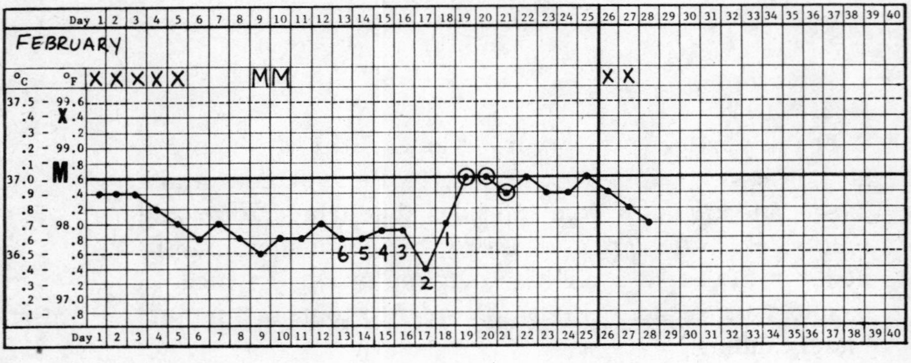

May 2

Dear Dr. Roetzer,

I was glad to hear from you that my cycle is normal and easy to interpret. In the meantime, I have continued taking my waking temperature and begun to pay more attention to the mucus symptom. I've enclosed my last two charted cycles and hope that you will again help me to determine the fertile time of each cycle. My fiancé and I want to thank you again for your letter; it has encouraged us to try this method of family planning.

MISS E.

CHART 22

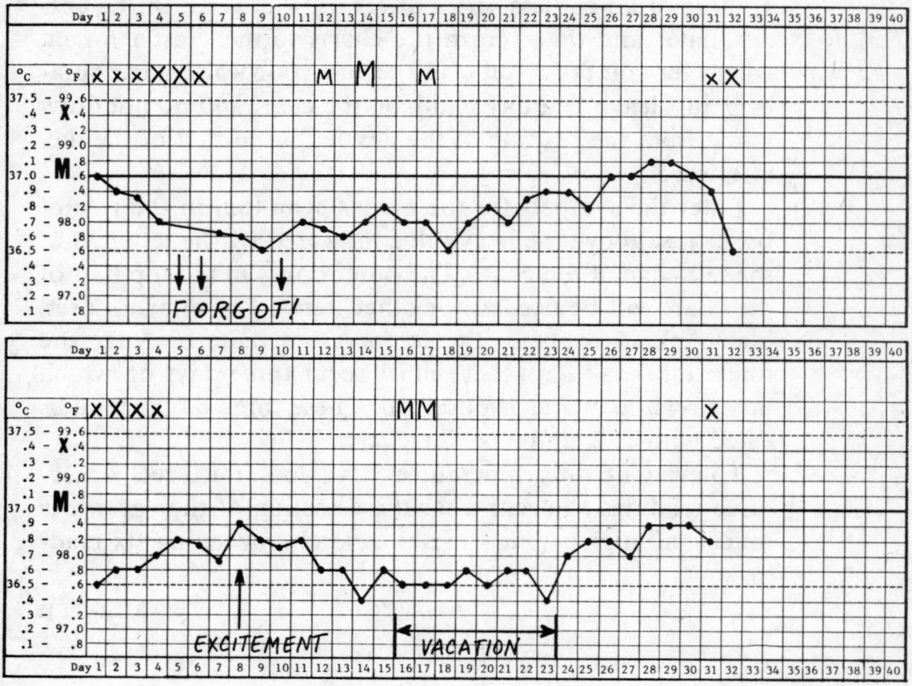

June 15

Dear Miss E.,

Your charts of cycles number 5 and 6 are enclosed. When I compare these with cycle number 4, I notice that the first day of your period in the 5th cycle would be February 23, but you forgot to put the date on your chart. Each day's date must be written on the chart in the box provided at the bottom of the column for that cycle day. Otherwise, how can you tell where you are in your cycle? Don't rely on memory! It doesn't work. Such careless little mistakes in charting are a prime source of surprise pregnancies.

Besides that, I can't tell what the date is for the first day of the 6th cycle; was it March 25 or 26? Here you see the beginning of an endless series of errors. Please fill in the correct dates and then return the charts to me. Lest I forget, whenever you fail to take and record your waking temperature, just leave that day blank on the chart and do not draw a line from the reading of the day before to that of the day afterward.

Enter the symbols for the mucus symptom in the row of boxes just above the heavy line indicated by the letter **M** at the left edge of the chart. The other boxes in the top half of the chart will be needed for other items. I have again used black ink to evaluate the temperature pattern. After the thick dot (peak day) there must occur three days on which no egg-white mucus is observed. These three days are indicated with 1, 2, and 3 on the chart.

To evaluate the temperature curve, look for three consecutive readings to occur after the cessation of the egg-white mucus, all higher than the immediately preceding six readings.

DR. ROETZER

CHART 23

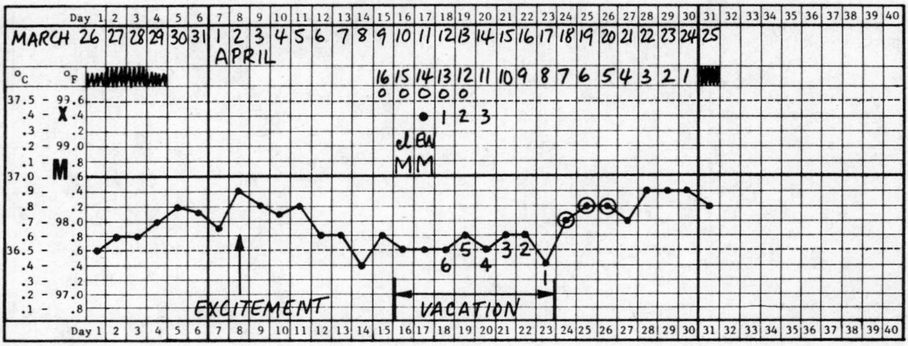

June 22

Dear Dr. Roetzer,

Thank you very much for the trouble you took to interpret my incomplete charts. I've been charting in duplicate, so I had no difficulty filling in the missing items for cycle numbers 5 and 6. I hope that I've done it correctly, this time.

Your instructions from Dr. Billings were really informative. As a matter of fact, I have rather neglected to make careful observations of my mucus symptom, but I plan to do that from now on.

I have tried to evaluate the fertile and infertile days of my last two cycles according to the advice you gave me. I used pencil to mark down my tentative judgements. I found that I had a potentially fertile time of up to 14 days in my cycles. I don't know whether I've calculated correctly, but the question will soon be acute, because we've set our wedding date for August 21.

CHART 24

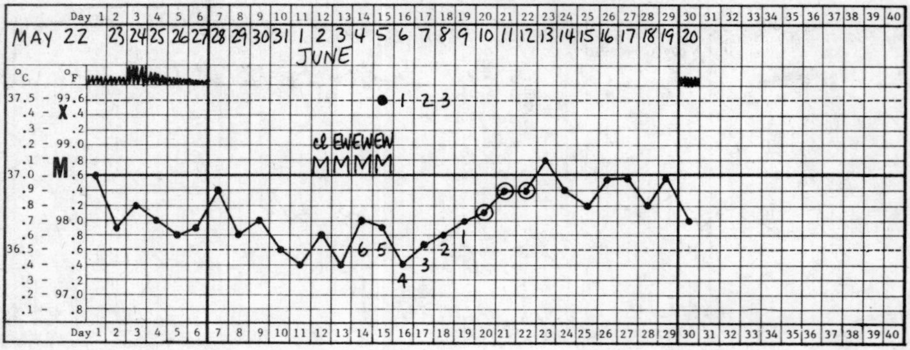

Again, we are wondering about whether to use this method or not. My future mother-in-law says that we're acting irresponsibly. My fiancé then suggested that perhaps I should take the Pill. As far as I'm concerned, I would rather stick with self-observation. We have both definitely decided to abide by the required abstinence during the fertile time. We've talked about it a lot, and we want to be supportive of each other in this effort. We will be living close to the university, so we'll have a somewhat regular schedule.

I've noticed that my temperature sometimes rises during the first parts of the cycle. For example, it was 98.4° F. (36.9° C.) on Day 7 of my 8th charted cycle. Does that have any particular significance?

MISS E.

June 29

Dear Dr. Roetzer,

Thanks to you for the valuable book! I received it today and read it carefully from cover to cover. I already feel a lot more confident about my own charting. I still do have a couple of urgent questions. Just a week ago, I sent you a letter with my most recent charts.

My first and most urgent question is this: What does it mean when my high-temperature phase is only 7 to 10 days long? You wrote about this in your book in great detail; I'm beginning to think that a few of my cycles were infertile.

Can I assume infertile days beyond Day 6 on the basis of my mucus symptom alone, which appears somewhat later than Day 6?

MISS E.

July 19

Dear Miss E.,

The charts you sent to me were well-done, and you also evaluated them correctly. I have left your notes for chart numbers 7 and 8 just as you wrote them down.

You have correctly noticed that the high-temperature phase has occasionally been too short. Dr. Vollman's studies have shown that such short high-temperature phases are typical for young women but gradually disappear as the woman enters the mature phase of her reproductive years. At the moment, you needn't worry about not being able to have children. I frequently see such temperature patterns in the charts of college students.

Your temperature pattern does have one peculiarity: It shows a delayed rise. After a little practice, once you have mastered the fine points of observing your mucus symptom, you need not wait for 3 elevated readings after the peak day, in order to determine the start of the infertile time. You will only need to verify the presence of a rising tendency in the temperature pattern when the temperature rise is delayed after peak.

Your temperature pattern clearly shows both a low phase and a high phase. It makes no difference if the temperature at the beginning of the cycle is somewhat high; it has a valleylike appearance, dropping somewhat lower toward the fertile time. This is what is essential! Since you intend to have a regular daily schedule, I'm sure you'll have no trouble evaluating your temperature pattern in future cycles.

If you are serious about wanting to avoid pregnancy during the first years of your marriage, you should start by assuming infertility only the first six days of the cycle. You may continue to send me your charts. We can then determine whether you can assume infertile days beyond Day 6 of the cycle.

DR. ROETZER

October 21

Dear Dr. Roetzer,

We got married August 21, and our marriage started with a long period of abstinence during our honeymoon. That did not help things!

On the basis of the mucus observations, we decided to have marital relations on the second day of encircled high readings.

MRS. E

CHART 25

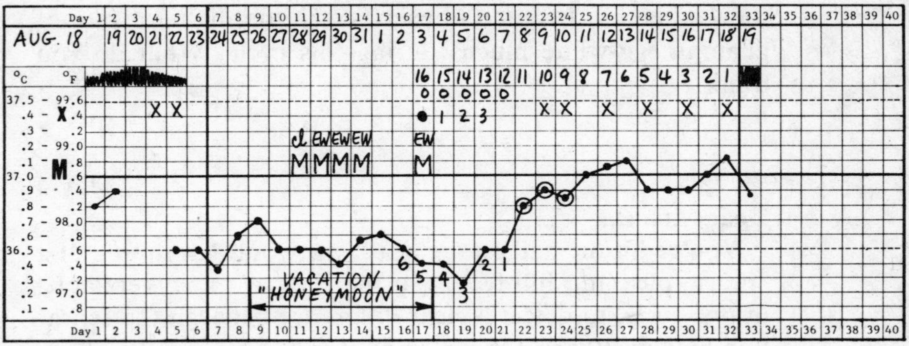

Note: Mrs. E. married in 1976 at age twenty-three. Both she and her husband were students at the time and felt they could not afford a child while they were still studying. But their attitude was one of willingness to accept a child, should one be conceived. Abortion was out of the question, as far as they were concerned. No pregnancy has occurred, as of this printing. Experience indicates that practically all such young couples are able to conceive within a very short period of time, once they actually decide to do so. So it is not a matter of the method working because the couples are infertile, as we sometimes hear said. Many young couples must postpone a desired pregnancy for five or six years through force of circumstance. During that time, they prove that young fertile couples can practice natural family planning successfully, and they accumulate valuable personal experience that will enable them to interpret their cycles correctly, even in particularly difficult situations: illness, stress situations, after delivery (particularly when breast-feeding), and then later, during the premenopause.

April 20
(Five months later)

Dear Dr. Roetzer,

We have had good charts for the last few months. I do have a question about my last cycle. On the 10th day of the cycle, I was able to detect a moist, pleasant, full feeling at the vagina, but I couldn't observe even the slightest trace of genuine egg-white mucus during this cycle. What do you think?

MRS. E

May 4

Dear Mrs. E.,

You've hit the nail on the head with your description of a "moist, pleasant, full feeling at the vagina." You were able, in this cycle, to detect a clear difference between the sensation on Day 10 and the sensation you had had on the previous dry days. That's good!

If in future cycles you notice no egg-white mucus on the days following the moist days, I suggest that you very gently insert your finger into the vaginal tract, to see whether or not you are able to notice egg-white mucus there. For your information, I have included some instructions for the internal self-examination.

I would very much like to hear your reaction to this suggestion.

I do hope that observing your bodily processes will not be a burden for you; I only want you to become more acquainted with yourself.

DR. ROETZER

May 24

Dear Dr. Roetzer,

Thank you for your further instructions regarding the external and internal examinations to be used when checking the mucus symptom. I find your suggestions very practical. I tried the internal examination right away, because I had already felt moistness. My curiosity turned into plain joy, for I was able to touch the cervix and its opening (it was slightly open). I could reach it easily with my middle finger, and the tip of the finger covered the opening. I also got just a little bit of egg-white mucus on my finger. That was May 9. On May 10, the opening was just about the same size. On May 11, it had widened, and I got a lot of egg-white mucus on my finger. On the next day, the temperature rose and the opening seemed to be even larger, again with egg-white mucus at the opening (this was in the morning). That evening, there was no more egg-white mucus present, and the opening appeared to have gotten smaller. The biggest surprise came on May 14, when I could scarcely find the opening. The only indication of the opening was a tiny dimple, surrounded by a soft, jelly-like mucus. The cervix was also firmer.

I rejoice that God gave me such a wonderful body! So does my husband.

MRS. E.

CHART 26

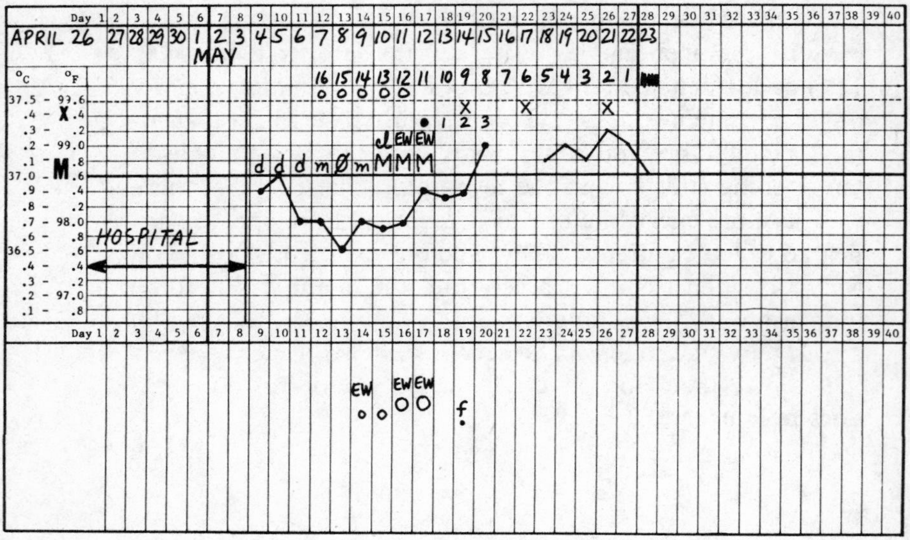

Note: Use the thick middle line to record your observations of what is externally present at the vaginal entrance. If your internal investigations of the vagina or the cervix show results different from what you observed externally, record these differences in the extra space beneath the temperature graph. Notice in the chart above that on May 9 only moistness **(m)** was observed at the vaginal entrance, whereas self-examination at the cervix resulted in a very little bit of egg-white mucus **e-w M** on the woman's finger. A soft and open cervix is charted with a smaller or larger circle, depending on whether it is open to a lesser or greater degree. The closed cervix is charted with a mere dot, as on May 14. During the fertile time, when the cervix becomes softer and more open, it sometimes also rises noticeably higher and becomes harder to reach. The chart illustrates all of this nicely: The circles become larger and are placed higher in the column. The small **f** indicates a firm cervix. Generally speaking, the cervical self-examination provides the most exact determination of the limits of the fertile period. No woman, however, need feel obligated to do self-examination of the cervix; every woman is free to decide for herself which observations she wishes to make. Readers interested in the information required for successful self-examination of the cervix are advised to read Dr. Josef Roetzer's book *Family Planning the Natural Way.*

June 22

Dear Mrs. E.,

I was particularly happy to receive your detailed letter of May 24, because I see that you have succeeded in making an outstanding personal discovery. Your description of the changes at the cervix during the various days of the cycle are excellent. In your case, it would be possible to rely solely upon the changes that you are able to observe by touching the cervix. An American gynecologist friend of mine, Dr. Edward Keefe, of New York, proposed such self-examination. He has traveled widely and has found that, in certain primitive cultures, similar observations of the cervix are self-evident and taken for granted. The discovery that you have made has been widely known and practiced in other parts of the world for centuries! I wonder, though, whether such a regular internal self-examination would be too much to expect from women in our own culture?

Your various observations now seem to coincide, so you might want to continue evaluating the mucus symptom in conjunction with the temperature pattern.

American natural-family-planning groups teaching internal examination at the cervix suggest that the observations be charted as follows: a dot = closed cervix
a small circle = slightly open cervix
a large circle = wide-open cervix

I suggest that you chart these observations toward the bottom of the chart and use the letters **f** and **s** to indicate a *firm* or *soft* cervix.

If you are confident you can tell which days are truly dry days, then you may consider these days also to be infertile. Inserting your finger just a little into the vaginal tract will provide additional confirmation of your initial impression of dryness, to help you to be certain that no cervical mucus is being secreted at the cervix above. Any personal experience that you have in observing the changes at the cervix during the early cycle days can be of help to you later in your marriage. The decision is, of course, yours, as to whether or not you wish to make such observations.

Unfortunately, most young couples deprive themselves of valuable learning opportunities. For instance, when they decide they are able to have a child, they generally want to get pregnant at once. It would be better for them to test the limits of their fertile time, to discover which days at the beginning of the cycle are actually infertile for them. To gain such knowledge requires, however, a period of experimentation, during which the couple might become pregnant, as they assume more and more infertile days at the beginning of the cycle.

DR. ROETZER

June 30

Dear Dr. Roetzer,

Thank you again, Dr. Roetzer, for your efforts in the field of natural family planning. We are very grateful to you. Your findings help us in observing the natural functions of our bodies and in using what we discover to our advantage. We also find that we cherish each other more, listen to each other, and seek our pleasure mutually, rather than selfishly.

My sisters have also begun to record their waking temperature. An older sister, already married, will probably be sending you her charts soon. My younger sister just charts to satisfy her curiosity.

MRS. E.

5

Thoughts Regarding Periodic Abstinence

"What do you think we are—animals?"

I once spoke to couples at a marriage seminar in New Guinea about the sympto-thermal method and asked the husbands who were present, "Is it really so difficult to go for a few days during each cycle without sleeping with your wife?"

"Of course not!" was the immediate response. "What do you think we are, madame—animals?"

"I once asked my father," the son of an African chieftain told me, "how he managed to space each of us children exactly three years apart! He said that in our tribe it was a mark of manhood to abstain from sleeping with one's spouse for two years after the birth of a child."

In New Caledonia, it was taken for granted that there would be no more marital relations after the birth of the second or third child.

"It is a little difficult," one man said. "After all, you are sleeping in the same bed with the woman you love."

For these men, it was a great emancipation to discover the cycle pattern of fertility and infertility in their wives.

"It's really hard for us. . . ."

"We've been using the sympto-thermal method for the last nine months and are generally satisfied with it, but the periodic abstinence, which sounds so romantic in your book, is really hard for us sometimes."

Dealing with periodic abstinence is part and parcel of the exercise of love involved in natural family planning. When you hear that the sympto-thermal method is unacceptable to a large number of couples, or that couples who use this method must have special motivation, what is meant is usually that periodic abstinence is not acceptable. No greater motivation is needed to observe the signs of ovulation or to take the waking temperature than is required for any other kind of contraception. Each method requires some motivation, whether before, during, or after coitus.

If intimate genital activity is the only possible means of communication within marriage, then abstinence is, of course, unbearable. If other means of communication are explored, a couple's mutual understanding will grow. Sexual intercourse will be experienced as a very special—but not the only—form of expressing love. Tenderness, longing, consolation, understanding, desire, warmth, security—almost any feeling can be communicated through our various senses.

In one of our marriage seminars, a young engineer told us about his experiences with periodic abstinence: "In our marriage, we find that each cycle has its time of courtship and its time of complete giving."

Couples who want to use natural family planning must accept and master the challenge of periodic abstinence. This can be beneficial for their overall marital happiness, precisely because there are ways in which love can express itself other than by physical union. It is often during these days of abstinence that true personal love may begin to really blossom. It can be a very meaningful time, especially for the woman, because she resists being only an object of sexual passion. A woman longs to be loved for her whole self. Just as the ocean tides have their ebb and flow, bodily love has its own timetable. "To everything there is a season. . . . a time to embrace, and a time to refrain from embracing" (Ecclesiastes 3:1,5).

Setting the Wedding Date According to Your Cycle

I wrote in *The Joy of Being a Woman,* "The young girl who has learned fertility awareness long before marriage will bring this knowledge as a definite contribution to her married life. The wedding date can even be set according to the cycle!"

An experienced natural-family-planning teacher from Australia sent me the following letter in response:

Ingrid, dear Ingrid,

NEVER! At least that has been my experience. No matter how regular a young lady's cycle might be, something can go wrong one or two cycles before the wedding. Strong emotions, stress, and tension can cause changes in the woman's cycle pattern. Our couples beginning their marriage using the ovulation method must discuss very seriously—prior to the wedding—the possibility of having a fertile honeymoon. Such a discussion can, however, lead to their first serious thoughts about natural family planning as a way of life—or, as I prefer to say, a way of loving—rather than a mere method of birth control.

Most people somehow have gotten the idea that intense sexual activity during the honeymoon provides the best foundation for future happiness. In actual fact, the healthy development of fantasy surrounding sexual love is often inhibited by unrestricted sexual activity. Young lovers often falsely believe that they know everything they need to about their spouses, without realizing clearly that marriage is a lifelong process of discovering each other more deeply.

Dr. Roetzer responded to the above letter, drawing upon his wide experience with couples in Central Europe.

A young woman who is thoroughly experienced in the observation of all her signs of fertility and infertility (cervical mucus and temperature) will not find her cycle pattern altered because of the excitement accompanying an impending wedding. Time and time again, young couples have succeeded in planning a favorable wedding date (assuming, of course, that they are free to select whatever date they wish). But circumstances often require the wedding to be scheduled for a date which, in all likelihood, will fall during the fertile time.

Dr. Vollman also frequently refers to the fact that the initial act of intercourse does not affect the normal variation of an individual's cycle range. He considers that to be a major argument against the notion one still so frequently hears: that intercourse, at whatever time during the cycle, is capable to bringing on an ovulation. ("Man is not a rabbit!")

Experiences That Speak for Themselves

A young student couple, still no children

Even though selective abstinence has its difficulties, I would not care to use contraceptives of any kind. The natural way of conception control gives every woman a chance to get to know her own body and its processes. You have to communicate with your partner and learn responsibility for your own sexuality.

A teaching couple, four children

Taking the Pill would be the simplest solution for me. I seemed to have no side effects from it, and as a couple, we wouldn't have any scheduling conflicts when it comes to having intercourse. I consider such a continuous assault on my body's natural functioning to be unnatural and unhealthy. Besides, periodic abstinence is an ideal way to keep sexual relations from getting monotonous. My husband is able to see my point of view, at least part of the time, and I try to make the challenge of periodic abstinence as bearable for him as possible.

A farmer and his wife, two children

I have been charting since the birth of our second child, about ten years ago. I also tried the Pill a couple of times, but regretted it and found myself returning to your method. There were too many side effects to every Pill I tried, including immediate weight gain. Once my dermatologist recommended the Pill to treat a skin condition that he thought was due to hormone imbalance. The first few months were very comfortable—no need to watch out for the fertile days—but then we started to get bored. A thing of beauty loses some of its attractiveness when it is available at any time without any effort.

A professional man, two children

I would like to say that I—I mean *we*—find your method the most effective and conducive to marital happiness. During the waiting period, we find ourselves talking things over more, and when the infertile days come again, we experience supreme joy in our sexual union with each other. There is a natural creative tension present that is missing when you take the Pill.

A physician's wife, two children

If a couple doesn't feel it's the right time to responsibly conceive another child and the husband abstains during the fertile days of his wife, he shows respect for the child they may later wish to conceive. As a woman, I find myself very much mentally and emotionally oriented toward the child that might be conceived from intercourse during the fertile days. Even without physical intimacy, I feel a deep bond with my husband and the child that could be.

My love for my husband grows stronger as I witness his love for this child, who he desires to come at the right time.

My husband's abstinence during the fertile time demonstrates not only his respect for my fertility, but also his reverence for the child that could be conceived from our physical union at this time.

During the infertile time, when a child cannot be conceived, I can open myself completely to my husband, concentrate entirely upon him, direct all my tenderness and warmth toward the man I married.

This reverence and respect for each other and for the child that could be conceived enriches our marriage and leaves us with a profound, quiet sense of mutual acceptance and understanding.

6

Sterilization?

Dear Mrs. Trobisch,

I recommended your book to my cousin, who at the time had four children. She now has five. She relied mainly on intermenstrual pain to tell her about her fertility. She admitted that she was careless about taking her temperature and that it was her own fault. Now she tells me she had her tubes tied after the last delivery, and that from now on, nothing can possibly go wrong.

My husband's opinion is that this was probably the best solution; now there's no need to worry about anything.

I don't feel I can quite agree with this. What bothers me is the finality of taking such a step. Once done, you can't undo it. Besides that, I'm not so sure it's God's will. We have to figure out now what to do ourselves. In three months, we're expecting our third child.

Dear Mrs. Trobisch,

My husband and I have two children, and we are expecting our third in a few months. We have discussed the possibility of a tubal ligation and both agree that we just do not want me to go through with this major surgery. However, my husband is not adverse to the idea of a vasectomy. In fact, he feels, as do many of our friends, that it is about time for husbands to begin sharing some responsibility for birth control with their wives. As I have always had extremely difficult pregnancies—both physically and emotionally—and a vasectomy does not bother my husband, why not let him go ahead with this minor operation?

These letters illustrate the situation in which many couples find themselves. It is a situation filled with contradictory arguments and emotions. To those who are lazy and superficial when it comes to coping with their fertility, sterilization offers a tempting solution—a no-risk answer that allows them to remain lazy and superficial. It seems like a clear, simple, and unproblematic way to be rid of the fertility dilemma.

The wife may hear a voice within, warning her. Filled with second thoughts and doubts, her conscience begins to bother her. Involuntarily, she senses that something is not quite right. Her maternal instinct tells her that although nothing can go wrong, at a very deep level, something is wrong and will stay that way for the rest of her life.

Many women pay little attention to this inner voice, or they even suppress it. They listen to what their friends say, their husbands, or their reason, instead of obeying their feeling for what is right. This inner voice often surfaces anew and makes itself felt after sterilization has taken place. There is seldom a chance to return. So it happens that a woman, even years after the operation, is overcome by a profound sense of guilt, sadness, and depression. The best of rational arguments cannot help her.

Her husband stands beside her, helpless to do anything for his severely depressed wife, but himself physically intact. Too late, he finds out that instead of a final solution, he has an endless problem on his hands. No pat answer is available. The problem remains. What is done cannot be undone.

Whatever went wrong cannot be made right now.

Is it any better for the husband who, instead of his wife, decides to go through with the sterilization process? Once again, we often find a voice deep within, whispering that something is, indeed, terribly wrong. While the choice may have been made for the legitimate reasons, the outcome may create far greater problems, both physical and psychological.

Second thoughts and doubts are found to appear as the husband comes to grips with the fact that he is no longer capable of fathering a child.

I still remember the thirty-year-old man who broke into tears at one of our marriage seminars when we showed the films about the birth of a child. He had gone through a vasectomy operation, hoping to save his marriage. The marriage did not last, and now he was newly engaged. While viewing the film, he was suddenly overwhelmed by the thought that he would never be able to give his new wife the tremendous joy of becoming a mother. God could never allow new life to come through their love.

Coping With Fertility in a Truly Human Way

As creatures of God, we are called by God to acknowledge and live with our fertility in a responsible manner. We are different from every other creature, because God made us accountable to Himself (*see* Genesis 1:26,27). We have a responsibility to nature, as well. It is disobedience to God, and unworthy of us as human beings, simply to allow ourselves to be driven to and fro, come what may. A sense of responsibility for our fertility demands that we not leave the origin of new human life to chance.

Sterilization: A Special Case

There are several ways of living with one's fertility. I have described them in my book *The Joy of Being a Woman.* Sterilization is, however, a special case, because it involves mutilation of the body itself, rather than temporary suppression or nonuse of a bodily function. Because it involves, in the majority of cases, an irreversible intervention in the life process, the sterilization decision is difficult to justify and needs more compelling arguments than any other means of avoiding conception.

Sterilization to Save Life: Responsible Mutilation

There is no doubt that sometimes a decision must be made that includes the loss of fertility. In making such decisions, it becomes clear that we no longer live in paradise. There is a rift in God's good world that extends to every realm of life, including our fertility. And so, let it be said openly, God's good gift of fertility may become a burden and misery.

There are sometimes weighty medical reasons that allow no alternative but to separate marriage and procreation from each other, though in God's creative plan, both belong together. Such cases will be few and far between and can be handled personally in consultation with a conscientious physician. When life is in danger, life may be mutilated for the sake of life.

Sterilization for Convenience: Irresponsible Shortsightedness

In recent years, sterilization in the form of tubal ligation and vasectomy have become popular, and society has misused what was once intended as a solution for only extreme cases.

A friend of mine tells of her experience at the hospital after the birth of their fifth child:

> After the doctor left, the nurse was taking care of me. As she was going about her duties, she casually asked me if there weren't "a little something the doctor still needed to do."
>
> My husband and I didn't at first catch the thrust of her remark. It soon became clear to us that she was referring to a tubal ligation, which is easier to perform immediately after delivery. With one quick glance to each other, my husband and I decided this was not what we wanted for ourselves.
>
> "Well, that's all right, too," the nurse nodded dutifully. "I just didn't want to forget anything."
>
> What struck my husband and me was how nonchalantly she made the suggestion, as if it were taken for granted that we would say yes. I'm certain that she didn't just make this offer after the birth of a fifth or sixth child!

Here there was no question of medical necessity; it was purely a matter of convenience. In such a case, sterilization appeals to the comfortable indolence of couples that do not want to bother with a natural, harmless way of avoiding conception—a way that may take a little more time and effort.

Let me make my point very clear: Sterilization for convenience is disobedience to the Creator. It is an intentional rupture of the intimate union of marriage and fertility, and as such will not go unpunished. So often one hears it casually said, "Why don't you just get sterilized, and then you won't have to worry any more?" That just isn't true.

Nothing Can Happen?

The first thing that can happen is that, despite sterilization, pregnancy can occur. One in a thousand women (sometimes even more) who have been sterilized will nevertheless become pregnant. It is so difficult to destroy the bond between sexual union and the origin of new life. Jesus' words apply here, too: "What God has joined together, let no man put asunder."

Five in a hundred sterilized women must reckon with postoperative complications requiring prolonged treatment. One in a thousand sterilized women will die, directly or as a result of some complication from the sterilization procedure. Six to ten percent of men who have had a vasectomy ask for a reversal of the operation, due to the death of a child or remarriage. However, these reversal operations are seldom successfully completed, and complications will often arise as a result of these operations. Even though these percentages are very low, these are *facts* that cannot be brushed aside. They are a quiet reminder that the precious trust we have received in our capacity to reproduce is not something that we may thoughtlessly dismiss.

A shortsighted decision in favor of sterilization can be costly in terms of the anxiety and sorrow that may result from it.

Many—particularly young couples under thirty—have little vision or ability to foresee the future. They do not really grasp what it means, never again to be able to have the child they may one day desire. As soon as a woman's tubes are tied and a man has a vasectomy, their choices are limited. Yet, if divorce or death of a spouse should result in a remarriage, they might again desire to have a baby, even though they previously were convinced that they would never want to conceive again. Or one of their children might die, which is one of the most traumatic experiences parents can have. Experience shows that bringing a new child into the world may be the only significant consolation for the parents' grief. Sterilization represents a sort of Damocles' sword always hanging over both the husband and wife.

Nothing dare happen to any of the children, now that the parents are sterilized. The price paid for this apparent peace of mind and feeling that "nothing can happen now" is heavy: the constant worry that something might happen to one's children.

Besides this anxiety, there is the sorrow that overcomes a man and woman when they begin to realize that something has been irrecoverably lost. Sometimes it takes many years until one sinks into the state of depression that is always bound up with a feeling of loss. Even if they don't admit it, they feel unconsciously that they are no longer whole and healthy. So a man and woman do well to listen to their healthy, instinctive tendency against sterilization.

Tubal ligation or vasectomy, as means of contraception, should be used only as a last resort by physicians. It is incorrect to tell patients that either method is 100 percent safe as a means of preventing pregnancy. I do not wish upon anyone the experience of having to listen to a young, previously sterilized man or woman begging to have the procedure reversed, so they can have another child. It is a tragic situation, and it does not happen all that infrequently. Anyone wishing to be sterilized must assume that the procedure will be irreversible. Even under the influence of the present sexual revolution, our reproductive capacity should not be a handicap to be gotten rid of as quickly as possible. It is, rather, a precious value that no one should give up without a great deal of thought.

A Wholesome Burden

Sometimes what appears to be quite reasonable on the surface is, in the end, unwholesome. What Paul wrote to the community at Corinth can be applied to the question of sterilization: "All things are lawful for me, but not all things are helpful . . ." (1 Corinthians 6:12 RSV), and a few verses later:

"Do you not know that your body is a temple of the Holy Spirit within you, which you have from God? You are not your own; you were bought with a price. So glorify God in your body" (1 Corinthians 6:19,20 RSV).

In light of these passages from Scripture, it may be said that whoever allows himself to be sterilized for convenience or for purely pragmatic reasons definitely does not glorify God with his body. What at first glance might appear to be prudence is, in God's eyes, stupidity and blindness. Gain becomes loss, and what seemed to promise health to a marriage turns out to be harmful. The words of Jesus are relevant precisely to this question of sterilization: "Whoever seeks to gain his life will lose it, but whoever loses his life will preserve it" (Luke 17:33 RSV).

No one denies that, in certain situations, fertility does appear to be very problematic. It is often a burden. But that is simply part of what it means to be human in a fallen creation. Technology cannot heal this burden or brokenness. There is no formula by which the world can pick itself up by its own bootstraps from its fallen condition. Technological manipulation will not, in the end, free us from our burden of fertility. Just the opposite. When we attempt to bring it totally under the control of human power and might, we only increase the burden of anxiety and sadness, of sickness, and even of death.

There is only one Person who can heal the rift in creation. It is He by whom the apostle says we were purchased at great price: Jesus Christ. He does not simply remove the burden from us; He promises to carry us, complete with our burdens. Once we realize that, we don't have to try to escape the burden by medical intervention. We can learn instead to live with it: "Bear one another's burdens, and so fulfill the law of Christ" (Galatians 6:2 RSV).

The burden is transformed, because our attitude toward it is changed. It becomes wholesome and healing, because it throws us upon Christ, letting Him carry us along with our anxieties.

Once pragmatic and utilitarian categories lose their grip upon our thinking and living, the burden of fertility can become a joyful gift. We begin to praise God in our bodies. How often have parents testified that it was precisely their unplanned, surprise child who gave them unexpected joy and a deeper experience of God's grace. One sometimes gets the impression that healing radiates to the whole of creation from the unexpected child whose conception was seen, at first, as a burden. Through these children, life—in a deeper sense—is able to come forth by God's gracious design.

Let us not forget that when God became man, He came as a child conceived unexpectedly.

7

Adolescence: A Time of Development

Miss B., engaged, wishes to postpone pregnancy during the early years of her marriage.

"Why doesn't it work for me?"

March 12

Dear Mrs. Trobisch,

It was with great interest that I read your book *The Joy of Being a Woman.* I am 21 and engaged. I was excited about trying out the temperature method, and my fiancé even prepared a booklet of temperature graphs.

Was I ever disappointed! It doesn't work for me at all. Just look at the graphs I'm enclosing. There's no clear temperature rise after ovulation—it just goes up and down all the time. The cervical mucus symptom gave me an idea of the approximate time of ovulation, but I couldn't see it for a whole week!

Besides that, I've always had very irregular cycles. How am I ever going to know the day of ovulation ahead of time? Do you understand that I feel letdown? Why doesn't it work for me? It's a lot harder to live with irregular cycles than to count off 25 or 28 days. But I would like to use this method. I don't want the Pill.

My fiancé and I want to get married soon, and we want to have several children, God willing. He still has three years of schooling left, so we must postpone having children for the first few years of marriage. It seems that birth control is presenting a problem for us, even before we've lived together. Things aren't as simple and romantic as I had imagined them to be when I was a little girl. What can we do? Should we see a gynecologist about my irregular cycles?

MISS B.

CHART 27

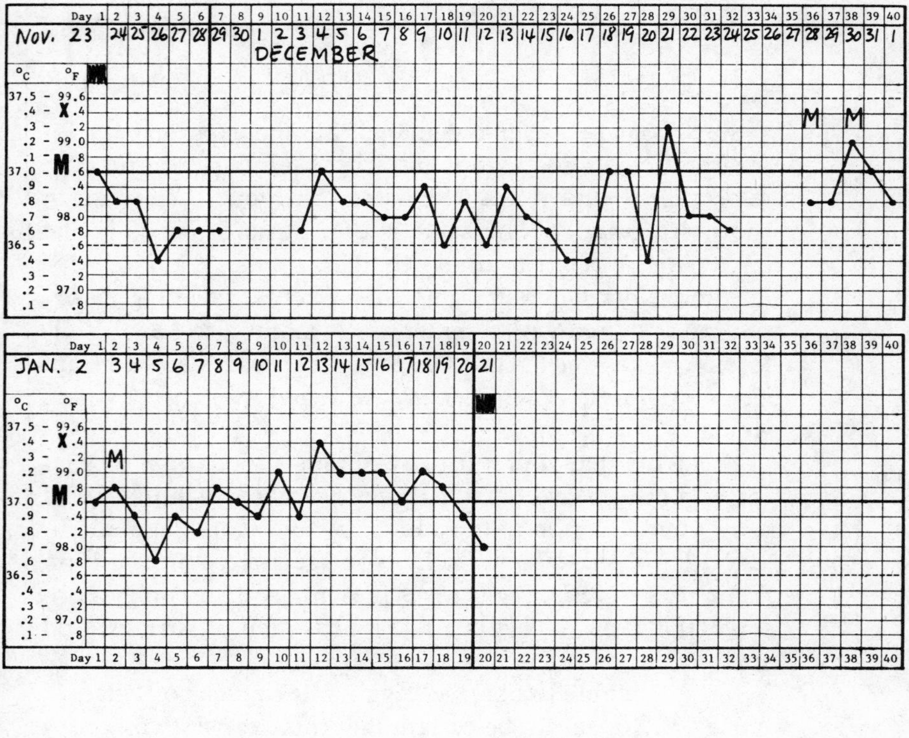

March 26

Dear Miss B.,

Your charts are quite typical for a young woman: Sometimes there is a very long cycle, in which the temperature seems to jump up and down without any rhyme or reason, and at other times there are cycles with very short high-temperature phases. Such temperature patterns can be viewed as a challenge to learn more about the development of your own body and how to observe and understand it better. I've sent your charts and your letter to Dr. Vollman in Switzerland and to our medical adviser, Dr. Roetzer, in Voecklabruck.

INGRID TROBISCH

Dear Miss B.,

Since you are a young woman of 21 who experiences a lot of stress and strain at work and whose job requires frequent relocation, I find it not surprising that your cycle pattern shows irregularity. The same is often true of coeds at the university. A better routine—by that, I mean regular sleeping and working hours and in particular, regular eating hours, combined with a better diet—might also have its effect on your cycle. Adequate free time and relaxation are also important! Also, you are still maturing as a young woman.

You write that your mucus symptom is sometimes present for an entire week. That is quite normal. I would like to draw your attention to the possibility of a more detailed observation of this symptom. Do you see any changes within the mucus secretion, when it is present? Are you able to observe the typical "egg-white" mucus that is stringy and stretchy?

If you are able to observe "egg-white" mucus or "glassy" mucus, then you can be certain that this egg-white or glassy mucus indicates potentially fertile days. Mucus of a different consistency may be present both before and after the days of egg-white or glassy mucus. Should this other type of mucus appear before the days of egg-white or glassy mucus, then you know that the potentially fertile days of your cycle are beginning and that the particularly fertile days of the cycle may soon occur. It is not at all important to pinpoint the time of ovulation! What is important is that in each cycle the woman be able to answer this question: When do my potentially fertile days begin, and when do they end? The very fact that you are taking care to investigate all these matters could result in a more regular cycle for you. I have seen it happen, time after time. Please be patient and keep charting. When your next cycle is completed, send the chart to me.

It is a very good idea to visit a gynecologist before your wedding, but it's hard to say what sort of treatment he will prescribe for your irregular cycles. Because you are still very young, it is possible that an untimely treatment would only result in disturbances in the observation of your cycles at a later date. I would therefore suggest that you see your gynecologist for an examination, to make certain that you are in good health, but wait to see whether your irregularity doesn't begin to take care of itself during the next few cycles.

DR. ROETZER

April 7

Dear Mrs. Trobisch and Dr. Roetzer,

I'm writing to let you know how happy I am that there's someone I can turn to for advice in this matter of birth control. You have proposed a method that I don't yet quite understand, although I find it practical and interesting. At the end of my cycle, I'll send you my chart for further evaluation.

As you know, my fiancé and I wish to marry soon, but will have to forego having children during the first years of our marriage. Sometimes I wonder whether it is egotistical to enter marriage under such conditions. Then again, should we really wait another three years, until everything is ready for us to have a child right away?

MISS B.

April 19

Dear Miss B.,

As far as I'm concerned, completing one's formal studies is a perfectly legitimate reason for a couple to postpone having children for a while. It's going to be a sacrifice for you not to have children, and apparently it will not be too easy to avoid becoming pregnant, with your cycles such as they are. If you are willing to take these difficulties in stride and to master them by self-discipline, I see no egoism in your decision to marry.

My wife and co-worker, Emmi, and I have discovered an answer for young ladies worried about their irregularity. A woman's reproductive capacity has its own life history, and its characteristics change as she passes from one phase to another. Trends in the temperature pattern reflect the changes in the woman's reproductive capacity as her cycling goes through its life history. Three phases can clearly be discerned:

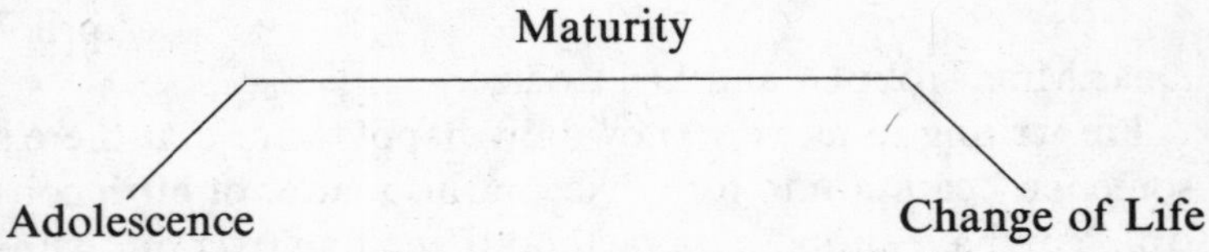

- Rising Fertility—This is the time of the adolescence of cycle history.
- A Plateau—This is the time of maturity and optimum fertility during her cycle history.
- Declining Fertility—This is the time of climacteric, or change of life, in the history of a woman's cycle.

Illustration 3

During my many years as a gynecologist in Switzerland, I developed the concept of the "gynecological age" of a woman. For the interpretation of a cycle, it is important to know a woman's gynecological age: that is, how long it has been since her first period (menarche). The date of a woman's first period is the start of year one of her gynecological age.

A 20-year-old who had her first period at the age of 15 is only 5 years old, gynecologically speaking. Another 20-year-old, who had her first period at age 9, however, would be 11 years old, gynecologically speaking.

When the temperature pattern of a young girl shows no temperature shift in the interval between two episodes of bleeding (*see* chart 28), the girl is still in her developmental years. She may be 20 and otherwise physically mature but still be on the way to maturity, as far as her fertility is concerned. Young girls still in the adolescent phase of sexual development will now and then show temperature patterns with but three to nine days of elevated temperature readings (*see* chart 29).

Reproductive maturity is not reached until a regularly recurring high-temperature phase of 10 to 16 days prior to menses is observed (*see* chart 30). This explains the apparent infertility of many young women, who are often able to achieve pregnancy only after two or three years of regular intercourse. If they have married during the adolescence of their fertility, they remain infertile, despite their adult age, until their reproductive capacity is mature. In the meantime, they only need patience, not medical treatment.

Great irregularity is also a sign that your sexual development is not yet complete. Medications and hormone treatments will *not* induce regularity; on the contrary, they simply postpone the development process and produce even greater irregularity. In no case should an adolescent take the Pill. The natural time her body needs to develop cannot be shortened artificially.

DR. VOLLMAN

CHART 28

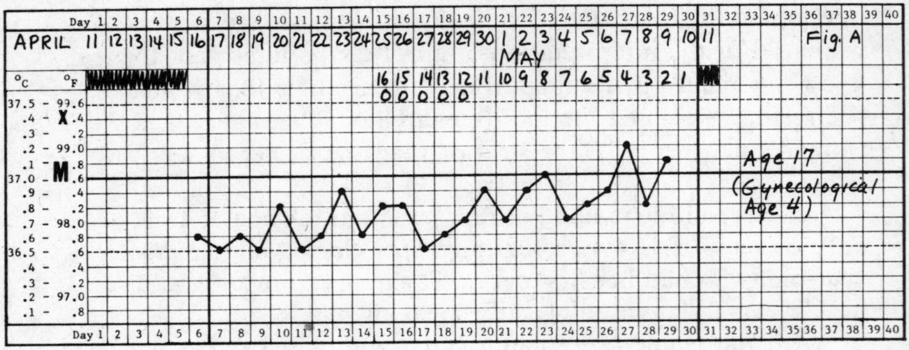

CHART 29

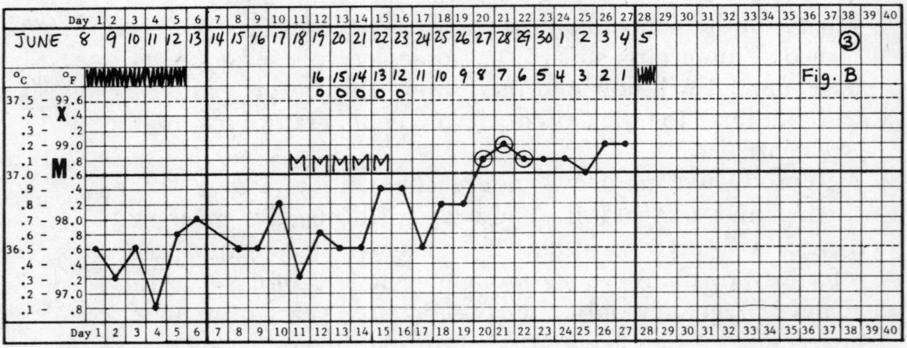

Note: During adolescence in particular the rise in temperature may be delayed somewhat after peak day—that is a trait peculiar to this phase of a woman's reproductive life. The short high-temperature phase indicates that the cycle was infertile, even though the interval between peak day and the following menstruation was normal. We can only guess at what actually happened in the ovaries (these more complicated speculations can be found treated in *Family Planning the Natural Way,* by Dr. Josef Roetzer).

CHART 30

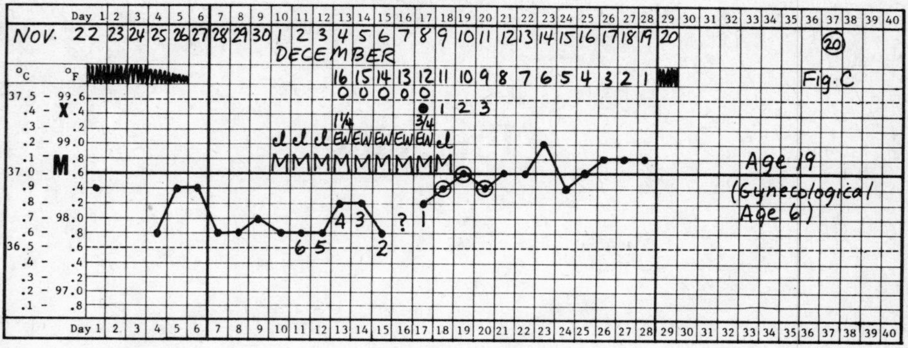

May 11

Dear Mrs. Trobisch,

After thinking a lot about what doctors Roetzer and Vollman had to say, I have come to the following conclusion: Insufficient sleep, the use of alcohol, false temperature-taking technique—none of these seem to be reasons for my cycle pattern. But frequent relocation could very well be part of the problem. Dr. Roetzer suggested that I send him my temperature charts for review: I'd like to get to the bottom of the problem.

Because of the uncertainty we face in the matter of family planning during my fiancé's remaining years of study, we have decided to postpone the wedding. In the meantime, I shall continue to chart my cycles. I really don't find it all that difficult, so it is not much of a sacrifice for me. In fact, I rather enjoy seeing the cycle pattern on my charts becoming normal.

MISS B.

8

Pregnancy

Mrs. T., housewife, lives dangerously

"Of course, if my husband will not restrict himself to the absolutely infertile days. . . ."

March 22

Dear Dr. Roetzer,

I'm sending you a couple of my charts for inspection. With regard to the "dry" days early in the cycle, I can honestly say that I am easily able to distinguish them from the "moist" days and from the mucus days, although I don't always bother to chart them.

My husband has not yet completely adjusted to natural family planning. I think he finds all this "calculating" too complicated, although I'm sure he could understand it, if he just took enough interest in it. There's no great problem—I try to diplomatically keep him informed about where we are in the cycle. Of course, sometimes I get a bit careless, as you can see from the enclosed chart. I might even be pregnant, but that's no great misfortune. I'm willing to accept the child wholeheartedly as God's gift to us. If I'm not pregnant, I plan to start abstaining during future cycles, as soon as the first sign of mucus appears.

MRS. T.

CHART 31

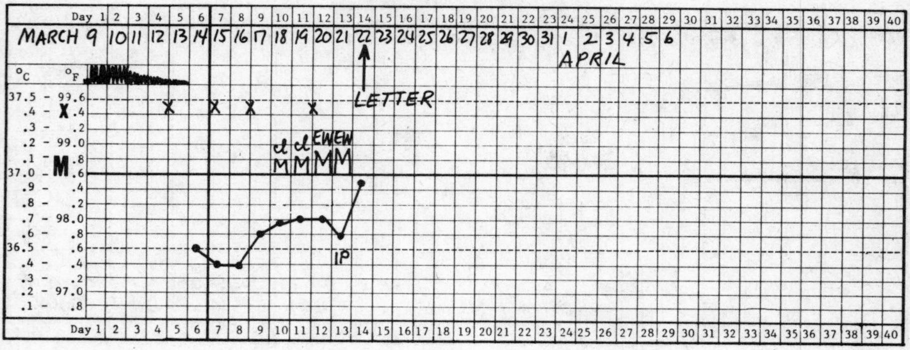

March 23

Dear Mrs. T.,

At this point it is impossible to tell whether pregnancy has occurred or not. I would very much like you to continue charting this cycle and to let me know what happens! I'm returning your chart at once, so you can complete your entries for the cycle.

DR. ROETZER

April 6

Dear Dr. Roetzer,

I've enclosed the chart that I previously sent to you. Even though we were together at the highly fertile time of the cycle, no conception occurred. I had already inwardly adjusted to the idea of being pregnant!

CHART 32

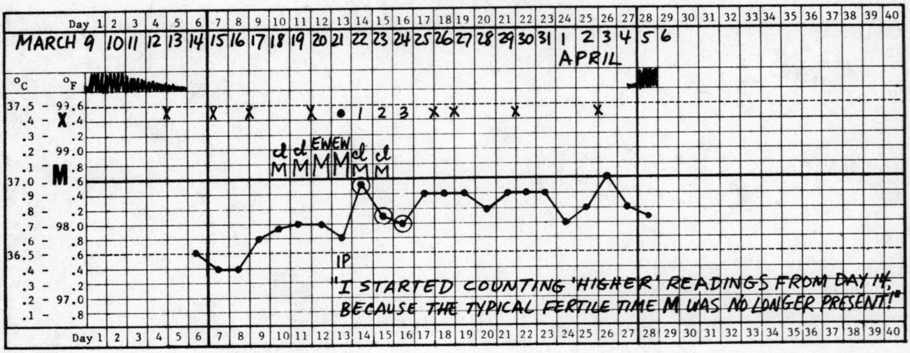

I carefully read through your instructions for the "dry" days. I don't believe that I need to make an internal examination; I have two or three days of dampness before the "egg-white" mucus appears, and feel that abstaining from the start of the moist sensation is adequate for us. I can do an internal examination anytime I feel uncertain. I pay more attention to the mucus sign than to what day of the cycle it is, although sometimes we have been a bit frivolous. Perhaps that in itself indicates something of my inner attitude toward having a baby. I would like to have another child sometime—another boy. Unless my husband is willing, I'll be satisfied with those we already have. Of course, if he won't restrict himself to the absolutely infertile days—which I shall always let him know about—he'll be to blame, to a certain extent, if he becomes a father again. He promised me he will take greater interest in my charting.

MRS. T.

Chart 33

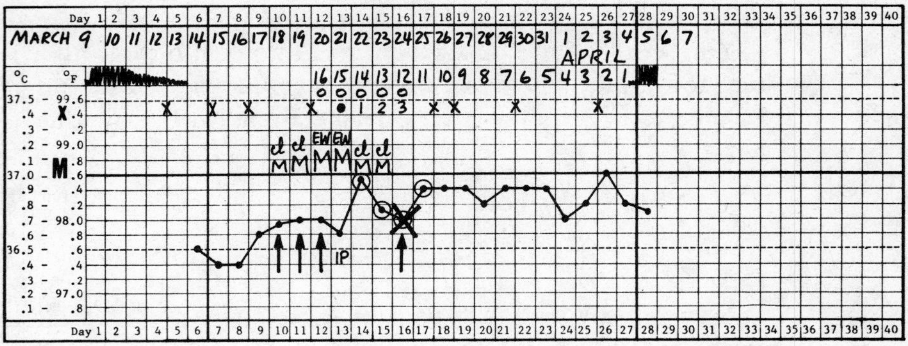

April 20

Dear Mrs. T.,

I have just received the completed chart of cycle number 5 and wish to thank you for your detailed letter.

You made a very good point in your letter: A couple should not automatically assume a certain number of days to be infertile during the early part of the cycle; they must instead take care to observe, as early as possible, the start of the mucus symptom. If you wish to assume any infertility beyond Cycle Day 6, you must take great care to do a good job of checking for mucus secretion. The mucus secretion might, in any given cycle, you know, start earlier than you expect it to. In future cycles, if the temperature should drop back to the low level after an initial rise, do not encircle the reading which is on or below the low level, as you must wait for one more high reading. Please note my marks on your chart. If the temperature remains at the lower level and does not rise as it did here on Cycle Day 17, then you must once again assume potentially fertile time.

Experience shows that pregnancy does not necessarily result from intercourse during the fertile time, but the outcome cannot be predicted in advance. You are quite right in resolving to hold more strictly to the rules for determining the start of the potentially fertile time.

You seem to have a rather relaxed and comfortable attitude toward the whole question of pregnancy, so you should be able to make your chart interpretations without undue anxiety.

DR. ROETZER

July 11

Dear Dr. Roetzer,

Now you can see my chart from cycle number 6. I wasn't really intending to get pregnant. I think that I assumed ovulation had occurred earlier than it really did. "You're safe now," I told myself on the morning of the third day after peak. I didn't pay any further attention to the matter until about Cycle Day 30, when I noticed that my temperature was still high and my period had not yet started. I do believe that I'm pregnant again.

I have to admit that if we really didn't want another child yet, we should have waited a few more days before resuming sexual relations. But, as I wrote in a previous letter, I more or less secretly wanted to have a baby, even though we had no intention of attempting to achieve pregnancy. My husband is taking it all very well.

I am looking forward to the future with confidence and plan to send you my charts after our child is born.

MRS. T.

CHART 34

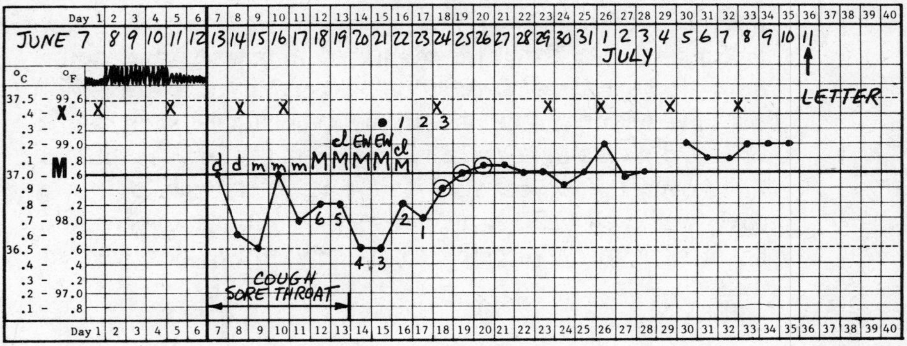

July 16

Dear Mrs. T.,

You are quite right. You did assume infertility too early when you used Cycle Day 18 of your cycle. Just two days had passed since the peak day, and besides that, Cycle Day 18 was only the first day of elevated temperature readings. If you wish to avoid pregnancy in the future, you should wait for the third "higher" temperature reading; that is, for the 3rd reading that lies after the peak.

I would like to make a further comment. With the first sensation of increased moistness, the "dry" days are passed and infertility may no longer be assumed. Intercourse on Cycle Day 10 of this cycle was quite risky; you assumed too many infertile days at the beginning of this cycle, as well.

Yes, of course, send me your postpartum charts. Best wishes to you during the coming months, and do send me a short note sometime, to let me know how you're doing.

DR. ROETZER

August 20

Dear Dr. Roetzer,

I'm now into the third month of pregnancy and doing fine. My husband is also happily expecting our child.

I have an appointment with my gynecologist soon, and I can hardly wait to hear the baby's heart beating. As soon as I discover I'm pregnant, I adjust to it at once, and I've cherished each child from the very beginning. Every child has a right to be accepted completely and to be loved, as well.

MRS. T.

Mrs. A., housewife, chooses a home birth because she dislikes the separation of mother and child that occurs in a hospital setting.

"This time we just let it happen. . . ."

November 15

Dear Dr. Roetzer,

This time we just let it happen. About the end of June, we were expecting our third child. We're happy that the third will be a good two years younger than our second and not as close as the first two were. Also, we believe it best that our two little ones have a third sibling, when it comes to settling disputes.

Of course, beyond these rationalizations, our feelings about the pregnancy are a mixture of joy and doubts, trust and worries, thanksgiving and supplications.

MRS. A.

CHART 35

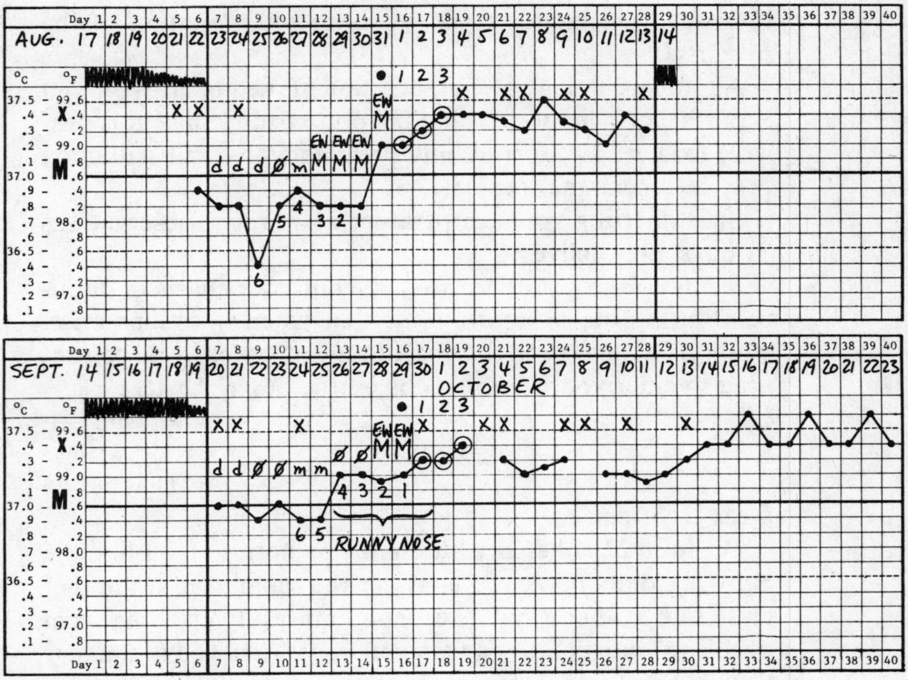

June 4

Dear Mrs. A.,

May I congratulate you on your evaluation of your last two cycles. You encircled only the elevated readings that occurred after the cessation of egg-white mucus and were not deceived during the second cycle by the premature temperature rise occasioned by a head cold. These charts are very instructive. They demonstrate how a slight indisposition can create the appearance of a temperature shift, while the peak rule prevents an erroneous interpretation of the false rise.

As you are well aware, observation of the mucus symptom is particularly helpful during the postpartum, since it is possible for fertility to return and pregnancy to occur without a previous menstrual period.

Start charting your temperature and mucus observations 21 days after delivery.

It might be a good idea to make out your charts in duplicate during the postpartum, so that when questions arise, you'll be able to send the chart to me at once, while continuing to enter your observations on the other chart.

DR. ROETZER

October 25

Dear Dr. Roetzer,

On June 22, a healthy little girl was born to us. I had the baby at home, because I consider the separation of mother and child at the hospital to be unnatural. Everything went fine. The young children were, of course, amazed at the new little baby—it was a fantastic experience for the whole family. I am now happily nursing our infant daughter.

My temperature seems to rise and fall randomly, perhaps because I have to get up often during the night.

CHART 36

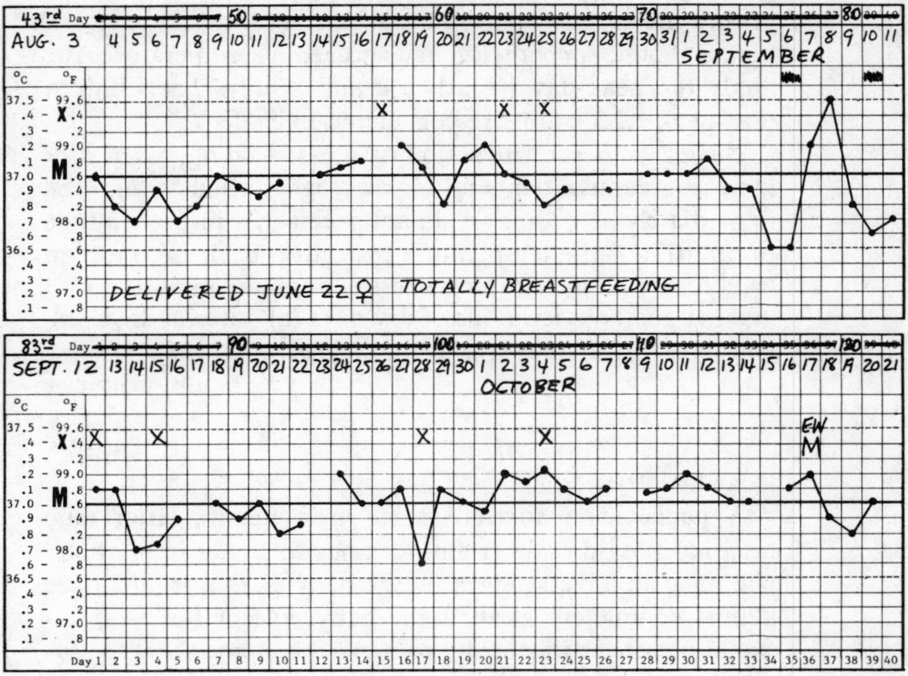

November 2

Dear Mrs. A.,

It is only natural that your temperature pattern will have little or nothing to say during the time of total breast-feeding. If you are, in fact, totally breast-feeding, without any supplements, you may assume infertile days provided that no mucus appears. It is very important at this time to notice whether, apart from the usual egg-white mucus, another kind of mucus can be observed, especially if it immediately precedes the appearance of the egg-white type of mucus, giving you advance warning. Up until the first appearance of any moist secretion, you may assume infertile days. If mucus should appear without a succeeding temperature rise, apply the peak-day rule. The **d** and ∅ days not within a post-peak 1,2,3 count are considered infertile.

During your present period of breast-feeding, a series of three consecutive temperature readings all higher than the immediately preceding six do not necessarily indicate a time of infertility—the temperature may drop back from a high level to a low one. I cannot stress enough the importance of making good observations of dry days **(d)**, interim days (∅), and days of moistness **(m)** or mucus secretion **(M).**

DR. ROETZER

April 8

Dear Dr. Roetzer,

A pediatrician advised me to stop nursing after nine months; he said that certain hormonal changes in my body will have an adverse effect on the baby. Is that true? I have almost completely weaned the baby, except for an occasional breast-feeding as she goes to sleep. I hope that the little she receives from the breast will not hurt her.

I have a few comments in response to your questions about the dry days:

• I definitely notice dry days immediately following my menstrual period.

• Seminal fluid is thinner than mucus and doesn't smell the same, but I do not feel absolutely certain about how to interpret my observations on the day after intercourse.

• For some time I've used internal examination to discern the onset of the fertile-time mucus; it's easy to do.

I've enclosed my cycle chart number 13. I am enthusiastic about learning more.

MRS. A.

CHART 37

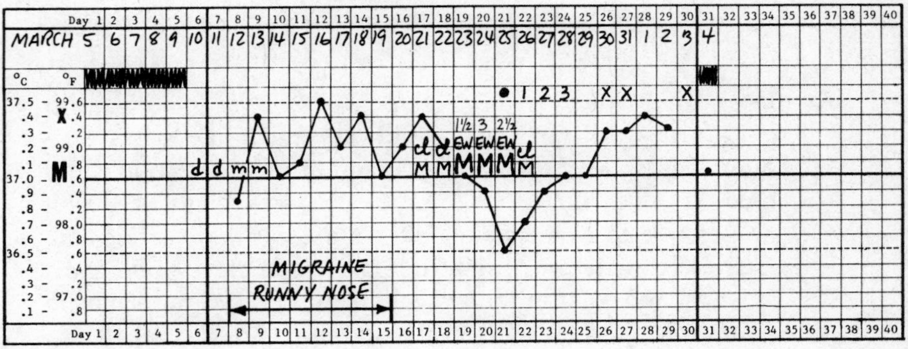

April 13

Dear Mrs. A.,

You did a good job of evaluating the potentially fertile time on this chart and noting the temperature rise, even though the high-temperature phase was somewhat short (that can happen during breast-feeding).

The temperature spikes at the beginning of the cycle are rightly evaluated in connection with the migraine headache and the head cold you had. You also did well to await the appearance of the mucus symptom signaling the actual fertile time after your initial sensation of moistness faded away.

Continued partial breast-feeding after 9 months will harm neither you or the baby. I suspect that the pediatrician you referred to had automatically assumed that you were taking the Pill; the hormones from the Pill do enter the breast milk and are then transferred to the infant when nursing. Otherwise, even prolonged partial breast-feeding will not harm your child in the slightest.

DR. ROETZER

Mrs. W. desires a child, but has only one ovary.

"I start crying every time my period comes. . . ."

March 15

Dear Dr. Roetzer,

I am now thirty-six and would very much like to have another baby. We have only one son, and our second child died. Four years ago, one of my ovaries was removed. Will it be possible to conceive again? We are getting worried, because we've tried for some time now to achieve pregnancy. My husband went in for a checkup, and everything seems to be normal. I start crying every time my period comes.

MRS. W.

CHART 38

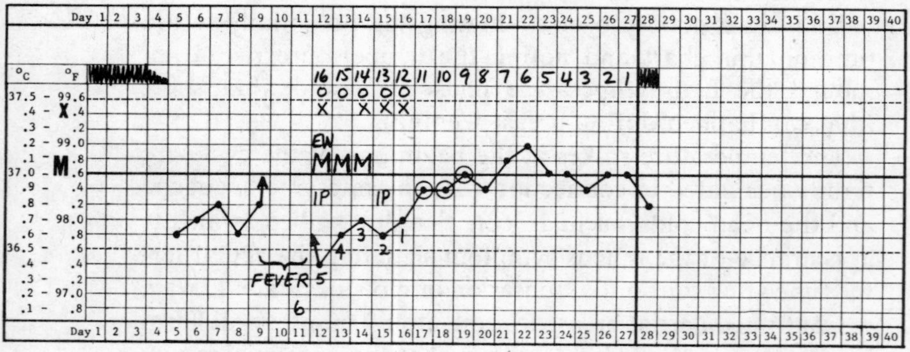

March 22

Dear Mrs. W.,

On the basis of the chart you sent me, I would say that conception would be possible. In general, one ovary is sufficient for pregnancy.

It is a well-known fact that a woman need not automatically become pregnant as a result of intercourse during the fertile time. In my practice, I have seen case after case of couples who were successful only after many months of trying to conceive.

I believe that an improved, more detailed observation of your mucus symptom would help you to determine the optimum time for conceiving. Try to see whether you are able to notice a "glassy" or "egg-white" mucus secretion. This egg-white mucus would indicate a time of high fertility. Abstain from the start of the cycle until about the final day or so of the egg-white mucus. This will take time and patience; you must first learn to identify the peculiarities of your own mucus symptom.

DR. ROETZER

June 20

Dear Dr. Roetzer,

Your letter was very encouraging. I become more and more disappointed. Until recently, the mucus sign always lasted at least three days, but on the cycle before last, I experienced only one day of mucus. I kept waiting for the egg-white mucus to appear, and then it was too late. The whitish discharge would appear that always followed the few days of mucus secretion. I do have one question, though. During the last cycle, I noticed a lot of thin threads present in the mucus. After a few hours, the threads were no longer present. During this time, I experienced a thick, swollen feeling at the vaginal entrance. For the most part, the feeling disappeared by the following day. Could these thin threads have been the sign of our fertile time? Please let us know!

MRS. W.

July 15

Dear Mrs. W.,

You've made excellent charts. The full feeling at the vulva, which you so nicely described, could be a sign of the fertile time. Women are so good at learning to distinguish sensations at the vagina that even blind women can use natural family planning. It seems to me that the sensation of fullness at the vulva could be helpful to you.

I know several couples who waited a good long time before they conceived, so take courage. I do hope that you'll have the patience to keep on charting your daily observations as you try to achieve the pregnancy you so earnestly desire.

DR. ROETZER

August 2

Dear Dr. Roetzer,

I have something special to tell you. The mucus symptom that I had observed in my previous cycles was apparently only a preliminary mucus secretion. On June 23, I accidentally noticed a little wad of mucus, clear as water, come out. Perhaps it was the last of the cervical mucus. By the time my husband arrived home, there was no more of it to be seen. In July, I paid very careful attention to the vaginal secretions. As you can see from the second chart, I noticed a little bit of this clear mucus on Cycle Day 13; then nothing for two days. Cycle Day 16 I felt moist all day, and the following day, early in the morning, the stretchy, glassy mucus was present. I thought to myself, "This time it'll work!" On Cycle Day 18, I could observe no mucus, but felt very dizzy. From then on I started to sense a tension in my breast nipples. I wondered whether I might be pregnant. What more can we do?

MRS. W.

CHART 39

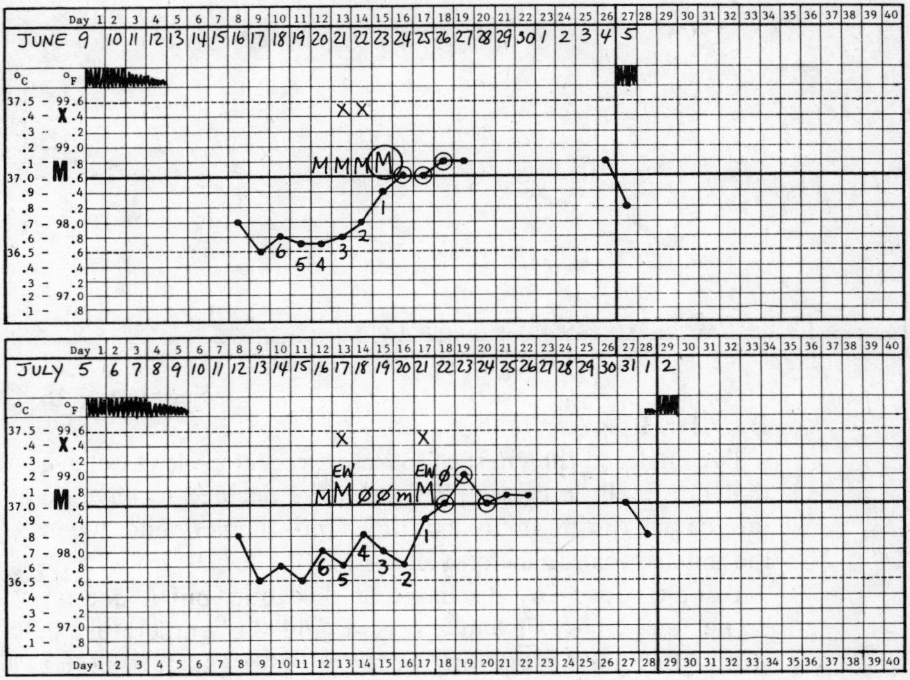

September 2

Dear Mrs. W.,

You have done a good job of filling out your charts and have made some excellent observations. I really can't give you any further advice, except to be patient.

Do you ever get the feeling that you are losing seminal fluid after intercourse? Sometimes it does happen. If so, put a pillow under your back as you lie in bed; this might slow down the loss of seminal fluid.

DR. ROETZER

CHART 40

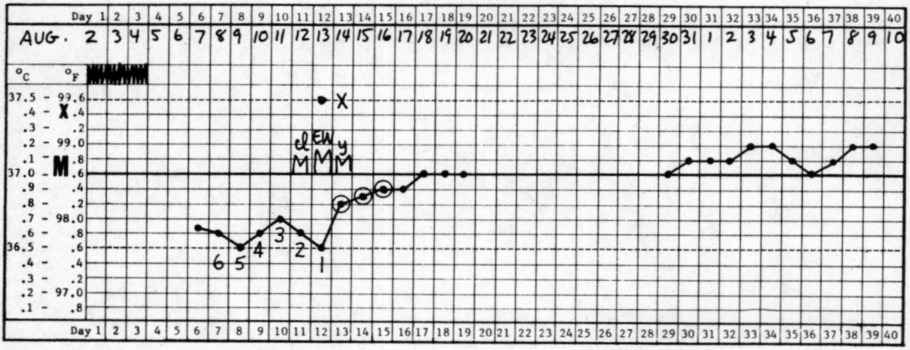

September 16

Dear Dr. Roetzer,

I've enclosed the chart of my most recent cycle. I believe that I'm finally pregnant. This time we decided to have no intercourse during the mucus days until the very end, when the mucus was somewhat yellowish.

I don't notice any discharge at this time, but it doesn't bother me. I haven't had a period, and the temperature is still high. I hope everything works out all right! If it hadn't been for my strong determination, we would have given up. Dr. Roetzer, thank you so very much. It was your constant encouragement that kept me from giving up. Thank you again!

MRS. W.

Mrs. F. deplores her unwanted pregnancy

"My husband would like to burn your book!"

February 3

Dear Mrs. Trobisch,

A few months after the birth of our second child, my husband gave me a copy of your book *The Joy of Being a Woman.*

We both read the book with interest and found, to our satisfaction, that the sympto-thermal method is indeed the most natural and most secure method available. Before we could put our trust in it, I took my waking temperature for two or three months and compared the figures with the charts in the book. Once I was able to determine that I, too, had a temperature rise immediately after ovulation, we started using this method, utterly confident that it would work for us. As far as intermenstrual pain goes, I couldn't depend on it much. The same thing was true with regard to cervical mucus observations, because I have so much of it. It lasts several days, sometimes right up into the first few days of the high-temperature phase. So I decided to rely upon the temperature pattern, and it worked perfectly, until about half a year ago.

Before we learned about the sympto-thermal method, we were using the calendar rhythm method. We really couldn't depend upon it and almost always had coitus interruptus (withdrawal). We have two planned children. We didn't want a third child—at least as far as my husband was concerned. He felt that in today's world, two children were enough for us, physically and financially. I guess he was right, and even though I always wanted a third child, I didn't want to force him into it. And then it happened—perhaps it had to be this way. In July I found out that I was pregnant, even though we had abstained as required by the sympto-thermal method; we couldn't understand how it happened. Just imagine how I felt. My husband was shocked and would like to burn your book! I was disappointed, not because of the baby, but because the method had failed us. It was the only method we could really feel secure using. Now we're not sure what we should do. I'm a very happy expectant mother, and my husband is happy, too, now that he has finally adjusted to the situation. But what are we going to do after the baby arrives? We would appreciate any advice you might have for us, Mrs. Trobisch.

CHART 41

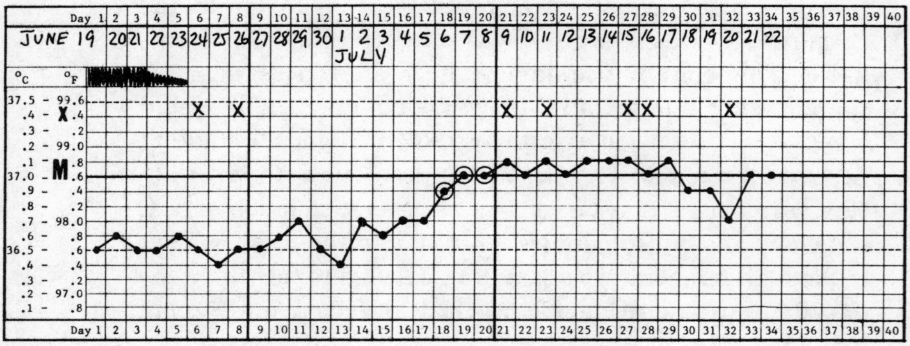

I've enclosed a copy of my June–July chart, so that you can see exactly what happened. Maybe there was something we did wrong or forgot to notice. Maybe it would have been better for us to wait a few more days, but who can say for sure? You say in your book that infertility is guaranteed from the third day of high-temperature readings. Please don't misunderstand me, Mrs. Trobisch. I'm not trying to blame you personally—nothing is further from my mind. I know that your book has really helped to make a lot of people happy. But in my case, something went wrong. There will always be exceptions—as you yourself wrote. Maybe I'm one of them. I would be most grateful for any advice and would very much appreciate your frank opinion about my situation. I resolved to write to you because I felt that only you would be able to answer my questions.

MRS. F.

February 21

Dear Mrs. F.,

Mrs. Trobisch, a longtime colleague of mine in natural-family-planning work, gave me your letter and asked me to answer it from the standpoint of a physician.

You wrote a very sincere and charming letter, and I hope you will not mind if I venture to ask you and your husband a few honest questions. The answers to these questions will be of importance to me in my research.

Please send me all your previous charts for inspection. You will, of course, get them back at a later date. The special characteristics of a given woman's fertility pattern only become apparent after several cycles of charting the temperature and mucus observations.

You mentioned in your letter that your mucus symptom sometimes continues into the first few days of the high-temperature phase. I notice that no mucus observations are indicated on the chart for the cycle in which pregnancy occurred.

It is our procedure to instruct women to learn to observe variations in the mucus pattern. This process of self-observation is not meant to be forced or strained, but as numerous women have found, becomes second nature after a while.

It is important for each woman to learn to identify *her own* particular kind of more-fertile-type mucus. Whenever a woman experiences an episode of mucus secretion containing this more-fertile-type mucus, she must consider the three days immediately following her final day of more-fertile-type mucus to be potentially fertile. Perhaps something like that would apply in this cycle. You said you had been paying attention only to the temperature, since your cervical mucus tended to persist into the high-temperature phase.

According to your letter, you used to use the calendar rhythm method, almost always having coitus interruptus.

May I now ask you a very personal question about the cycle of conception? What happened during this cycle? Both withdrawal and the use of a condom have a certain failure rate when used during the fertile time.

DR. ROETZER

February 26

Dear Mrs. Trobisch,

I now feel secure that, thanks to your help and that of Dr. Roetzer, I can learn to correctly identify my rhythm of fertility and infertility. It was clear to me, as I read your letter, that I had paid too little attention to the mucus symptom. That was our downfall in the present pregnancy. I had previously thought that the temperature pattern was more important than the mucus symptom. I didn't realize that with adequate mucus, sperm could live as long as seventy-two hours. I did not clearly understand that the infertile time begins only with evening on the day of the third high reading *after* the cessation of the mucus symptom, even though you had explicitly made that point on page 49 of your book. I still don't know how I missed that. I must have read your book at least ten times.

I recall that during the cycle in which I conceived, the mucus was still present on the second or third day of high temperatures. In fact, I even remember mentioning to my husband, "I can't understand why this mucus is still present after the temperature has been high for two days." My husband remembers my saying this, too. Unfortunately, I didn't enter it on my chart, because I thought it didn't make any difference, once the elevated temperatures had started. That was my mistake, and a big one, too. According to the rule, we should definitely have waited for three days of elevated temperature after the cessation of mucus. I have promised myself to study this all much more carefully in the future.

MRS. F.

March 15

Dear Mrs. F.,

You are quite right in assuming that you got pregnant because you still had an egg-white mucus secretion during the first two days of high temperature. I have charted the mucus observations you mentioned and identified the peak day with a thick black dot (the peak day is the final day of the egg-white mucus secretion). The rule to remember is: Encircle only those elevated readings that occur *after* the cessation of the typical egg-white mucus.

DR. ROETZER

CHART 42

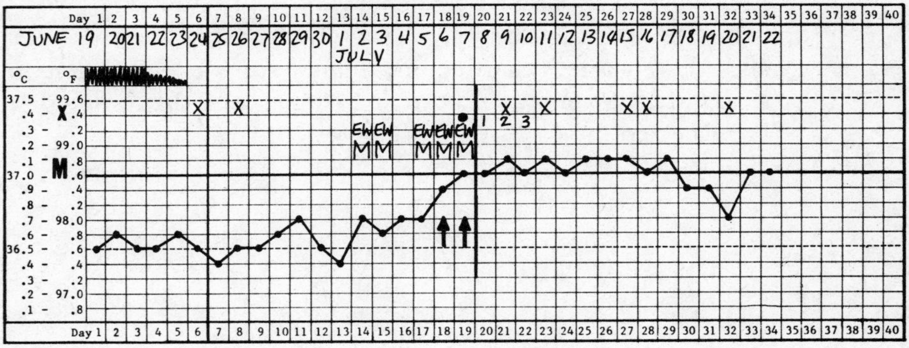

June 12

Dear Mrs. Trobisch,

We have experienced many beautiful things, and the most beautiful was the birth of our baby girl. Our daughter is now seven weeks old and healthy, and we are very, very happy. This delivery was quick and easy, just as with the birth of our previous children. What was so beautiful was that this time, my husband was able to be there, too. It was quite an experience for him, and he's sorry that he did not have the opportunity to be present at the births of our other children.

He apparently had a number of funny ideas about what a delivery was really like, and I know he was completely surprised and relieved to discover that it could all be so restful and painless. I'll never forget the surprise in his eyes, as he saw first the tiny head and then the whole human being making its entry into the outer world. His eyes were radiant with joy as the child was placed in our arms. We were speechless, overwhelmed with joy. I have never had such a beautiful and joyous delivery! Before, my feelings and my joy had been mine alone, but this time my husband and I gave birth to our child together. It was one of the most beautiful experiences we've had during our entire twelve years of marriage. We are so happy and thankful to have been able to experience it once again. Only now have we really become a "family." Two children are not really enough. I started charting my temperature exactly three weeks after the baby was born and plan to send the charts to Dr. Roetzer.

MRS. F.

9

Postpartum

Mrs. S., recently delivered, is just learning how to chart
"We're all very happy. . . ."

May 30

Dear Dr. Roetzer,

I was delivered of a healthy boy yesterday. We're all very happy. Three weeks from now, I'll begin charting according to your instructions. I'm glad you'll be available to answer my questions while I'm learning how to chart. I plan to totally breast-feed as long as possible.

At first, I'll have to be getting up quite a bit at night to care for the baby. My mother will help with the housework, so I can devote all my energy to the children.

I'm looking forward to the future with confidence and would appreciate any help you might be able to provide.

MRS. S.

June 10

Dear Mrs. S.,

It is particularly important during the postpartum to make daily observations of the mucus symptom. Start charting your observations three weeks after delivery. If at first you should have some difficulties, remember that this is a gradual learning process.

You are, of course, aware that your fertility may return even prior to your first postpartum menstrual period. If you begin charting your temperature and mucus signs three weeks after delivery, you should be able to recognize these fertile days in time. The experience of other women has shown that, by a combination of temperature and mucus observations, the potentially fertile days can be very nicely identified. This holds true even though you may have to rise during the night to care for your infant.

During the postpartum, I recommend that you make out your charts in duplicate. That way, you can send one of them to me at once, if you have any questions, and you can continue to chart your observations on the other.

DR. ROETZER

August 30

Dear Dr. Roetzer,

Thank you for the materials! I'm sending you my charts and await your evaluation of them, as well as any further advice. I hope that I'll catch on to this method in the course of time. Meanwhile, I would like to continue our correspondence.

I should mention that I was able to breast-feed totally only for the first three weeks. Then the milk supply diminished, so I continued three more weeks with partial breast-feeding.

MRS. S.

CHART 43

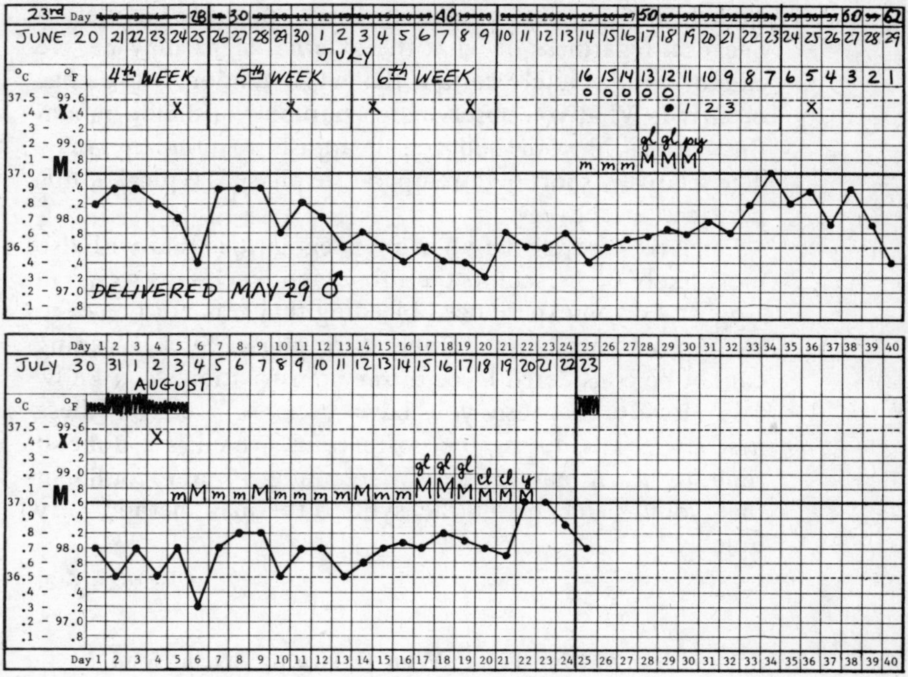

Note: On this chart, the symbol **py** means pale yellowish, thin secretion; **y** means a definite yellow, more lumpy, thicker mucus.

Dear Mrs. S.,

You did a beautiful job of charting. The chart you sent shows a pattern that is typical for postpartum. You did know that the first six weeks after delivery are infertile days for the nonlactating or partially lactating mother. The mucus symptom, which appeared during the seventh week postpartum, just after you stopped nursing, indicates the approach of a possible ovulation. I say "possible" ovulation because, regardless of what the external signs may be, we cannot be absolutely certain that an ovulation will or has occurred. What you observe are symptoms of the hormonal fluctuations in your body, as it adjusts to nonpregnancy. The relatively short high-temperature phase is typical of this period after delivery.

The second cycle shows some irregularities that will also most likely be present in the subsequent cycles, as well. On August 23, you experienced bleeding that was not preceded by a pronounced high-temperature phase. Such bleeding cannot be considered to be a *true* menstruation. You know this already. Because you have done so well on these first few charts during the postpartum, which is a difficult time to learn natural family planning, I am confident that you'll catch on to the sympto-thermal method very quickly.

DR. ROETZER

First Aid for Those Who Desire to Breast-feed

Many mothers would like to totally breast-feed their infants but stop after a short time because they think they don't have enough milk. My advice is: Keep the baby at the breast! The baby should be given the breast frequently; at first, this means at least every two hours. The child's sucking will cause the mother's body to produce an appropriate amount of milk. At each feeding, the baby should be given both breasts, starting with the right breast for one feeding, then the left at the next feeding, and so on. If, in addition, the baby is given the bottle, it will suckle less and less at the breast, because the bottle does not take as much effort, and the mother's milk in turn will diminish.

Total breast-feeding means the baby's total nourishment comes from the breast. No supplements are allowed, not even tea or other liquids. There should be at least one feeding during the night. No pacifier, other than the mother's breast, should be given to the baby. The whole family should see to it that the mother has a chance to nurse the baby in peace and quiet, because when the mother fully relaxes, her milk tends to flow by itself.

"Breast-feeding: a time of self-discovery. . . ."

October 29

Dear Mrs. Trobisch,

Thank you very much for the book *The Joy of Being a Woman.* Despite all the extra work I had to do while we were moving, I took time to read the whole book. What interests me most at the present is the section on breast-feeding. A lot of people are surprised that our baby is still nursing (it's only three months old).

A mother who wants to breast-feed can easily lose heart in today's hospitals, where the atmosphere is often hostile toward breast-feeding. I faced opposition from hospital personnel at the birth of each of our children. When things didn't go perfectly from the start with my nursing, I would be told to forget it, because once I got home and was up and about, I wouldn't have time for it, anyway. Just the opposite was the case!

At the hospital, I couldn't convince them not to give the baby any supplements, but was able to take care of that after my experience with my first child. At each feeding, I would give the baby both breasts (even at the hospital), starting one feeding at the right breast and the next at the left breast, and so on. After my most recent delivery, I couldn't get the milk ducts on one side to loosen up, so I asked for the breast pump. I had to make several requests before I finally got the pump. A mother less well prepared than I might simply have given up.

I strongly believe that without a real desire to breast-feed and without the right attitude toward the infant, it is impossible to breast-feed. At first you do need quite a bit of time. What is the extra effort, by comparison with what you receive in return? With the present baby, I have experienced most keenly how the time spent in breast-feeding is, for me, my sole opportunity for rest in the midst of otherwise incessant confusion and work. For the baby, it is a time of self-discovery and unhampered bliss. Without breast-feeding, I would never be able to have such profound contact with my child.

I have almost decided to start promoting breast-feeding in my own community, whenever the opportunity presents itself.

MRS. B.

"Your child or your husband?"

June 13

Dear Mrs. Trobisch,

As I look back over a prolonged period of breast-feeding, I sense how wonderful the whole time was for me. During the first 4½ months, I was totally breast-feeding. Then, as I introduced supplements, I continued to offer the breast whenever the baby wanted it, and that was still quite frequently.

There was only one drawback. For months I had no menstrual period and was unable to tell when ovulation was occurring. I never knew where I was in my cycle.

My husband and I had long periods of abstinence during these months. I'm very pleased at how much patient understanding he showed me during this time. It really wasn't very easy.

I would like to recommend breast-feeding to a friend of mine, but am nervous about doing so, because of the abstinence involved. I don't know whether she and her husband would take it; it might harm their marriage.

How can you get through the period of breast-feeding

without prematurely disturbing the close mother-child relationship by another pregnancy and without burdening your relationship with your spouse by long periods of abstinence? After all, a strong, intimate relationship with one's spouse is one of the most important requisites for successful breast-feeding.

Mothers who totally breast-feed their newborn infants are often without menstrual periods for months after delivery, so they can't tell when they're ovulating.

Is there any good way to get through this difficult time?

MRS. B.

June 27

Dear Mrs. B.,

Thank you for your frank letter. I am glad that you are still able to breast-feed, despite difficulties. Rest assured: Your own milk is the very best nutrition you can give your child. Nothing can substitute for it.

A mother who is really *totally* breast-feeding can be certain of infertility for the first twelve weeks of postpartum. She will be able to give herself completely to her husband during this time, to show her love and gratitude to the man who is, after all, the child's father. In giving herself to her husband, she will experience, along with her child, a sense of fraternal protection and security. Her husband will also be at peace. Numerous couples will testify that these three months are one of the most precious times in their married life.

With a good, exact observation of your mucus symptom, you should be able to succeed in determining your infertile days. I have enclosed a chart from a young breast-feeding mother who used the peak-day rule to evaluate the potentially fertile days while nursing.

CHART 44

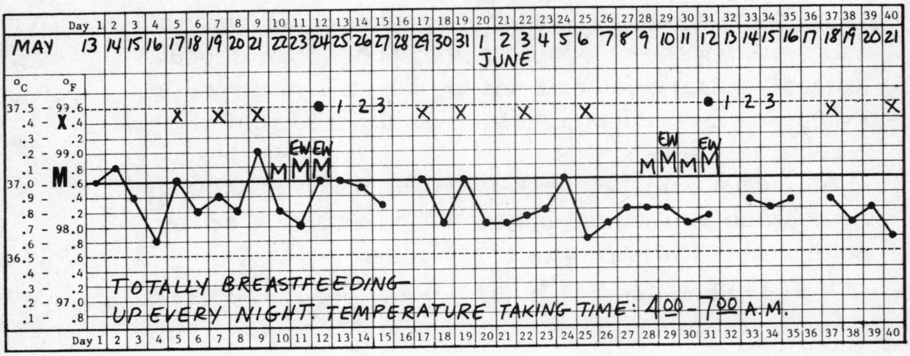

Enclosed, you will find the testimony given by one young couple. In it, they give their answer to the question that you yourself posed: Is the abstinence required during weaning impossible to bear?

"We didn't think so. It naturally demanded a lot of patience and understanding, as well as lots of love. That means love expressed by a lot of tender gestures, and not just in word. We tried to show our desire for each other by bodily contact and touching, all the while remembering that there would be a tomorrow, when this time of abstinence would be over. We decided to undertake this Lenten fast, and we believe that couples who make a similar decision, based on shared faith and love, will achieve a state of creative abstinence that leads to spiritual enrichment in marriage. The nursing mother who feels surrounded by such love need not worry about whether to give herself to her child or to her husband. She is free to give herself to both."

INGRID TROBISCH

"*We* are going to breast-feed *our* baby!"

Dear Mrs. Trobisch,

It is important for a young mother to realize that her husband stands 100 percent behind her decision to breast-feed. Conditions at the hospital tend to discourage a woman from breast-feeding and to make her feel as though she won't be able to succeed at it. But she will be able to, if she just knows that her husband is not jealous and that he really does want her to be able to breast-feed their baby. That's my experience.

Of course, there will be some difficulties at first. If your husband is there to cheer you on and keep you going, you won't falter. It takes a lot of time to get started with a newborn infant. You have to lie down: You need extra time to rest. My husband was the only one who could give me that. When I told him, "I just can't do it," he would say, "No, *we* are going to breast-feed *our* baby!" Every time I finished nursing the baby, he would thank me for having fed her such a nutritious meal.

What does breast-feeding mean to a woman?

"I finally grew up. . . ."

Dear Mrs. Trobisch,

I was able to breast-feed our third child for eleven months. In retrospect, I see how important this whole time was for me. I discovered something that I had never learned during the previous thirty-one years of my life. Whenever I put the infant to my breast, a nagging question would recur: Do I really have enough milk? As I saw this child of mine grow and blossom, I began to trust in myself, to trust that I could give my child everything he needed. I experienced how surely the milk began to come, as certain as day follows night. It was a crucial experience: acceptance, passivity, serenity. I developed a deep sense of trust as a result of this experience of my capacity to breast-feed; I began to realize that I, too, will receive whatever I need. My whole personality has changed. I no longer fret about what I should say and what I should do when I am with others. I have become more sure of myself. Others have noticed the change in me, too. They tell me that I have finally grown up.

"I became very quiet and felt completely at peace. . . ."

May 15

Dear Mrs. Trobisch,

Dominic was a Down's Syndrome baby, sickly at birth, and was only a day old when they took him to a special children's hospital for treatment. In spite of everything we've gone through, Dominic was and remains for us a great blessing. God our Father has carried both him and us through that initial period of sorrow.

Being able to breast-feed him helped out, too. Just the feeling that our baby was getting milk pumped from my breasts made me feel as though I were able to do something about it all. And so, while the lady in the bed next to me was nursing her child, I was vigorously pumping my breasts, despite the protest of the nursing staff.

Four weeks later, we were able to take our little darling home. He had never before suckled at the breast, and my milk supply was just enough for two or three feedings. I received no encouragement whatever from the hospital staff, and, somewhat nervous, put Dominic to the breast anyway. Immediately he drank to his heart's content. He rejected the bottle—he even broke one—and he forced me to total breast-feeding, even though my milk supply was insufficient. I spent one whole day with a hungry tot crying at the breast, before milk finally came. Then he was satisfied. We didn't need scales to tell us that our baby was growing. But our joy was short-lived. Medication that I needed caused the milk supply to diminish, and I underwent further surgery when Dominic was but eight weeks old. Every physician I talked to recommended that I wean the baby at once. Happily, our concern for Dominic and my stubbornness won out. I pumped the milk from my breasts once again and threw it out (I was full of medication). At home, Dominic was drinking at most one or two ounces at mealtime, and it was a thin, pale baby that greeted me when I returned from the hospital. The first morning I was back, he suckled greedily at the breast and drank almost seven ounces!

After hurdling all these obstacles, it meant a great deal to me to enjoy untroubled nursing, to lay my contented child in his little bed. I myself became very quiet and felt completely at peace at the end of the day, knowing that I had been able to give this tiny child everything it needed.

Besides that, there really is nothing more practical than breast-feeding. We were always on the go—doctor's appointments, treatments, and so on. Dominic had to endure much, but no matter where we were, he could always find rest at my breast. When he was three months old, he had to have physical-therapy treatments four times daily. It was just as hard for us as it was for Dominic, with all his screaming and crying. He and I both found our consolation as he nursed at my breast.

Breast-feeding was the only thing that helped him when he had a fever; he refused to take the prescribed medication or to eat his special diet. I don't know how I could otherwise have gotten this tiny, whimpering patient to be still, had it not been for God's gift of mother's milk for His little ones.

Dominic went for almost an entire year without any illness, was able to eat with a spoon and drink from a cup, and at fifteen months of age, got his first teeth. He made friends with other children and suddenly had more exciting things to do than to be at his mother's breast. He became more independent. Evenings, all we had to do was sing him a song and he would settle down.

I am glad that I was able to breast-feed for those sixteen months, and I am thankful to all who encouraged me to continue. Despite all the initial hardship, it was worth it.

10

Premenopause: Threshold to a New Life

For those couples who have not "cut out" their fertility through sterilization (Dr. Paul Marx calls this the "barnyard approach"), premenopause can be one of the most difficult times for them to live in harmony with their fertility. Only in rare cases will there be couples who may have married late and therefore seek to have children during these years. By the way, the assumption that a mother who is over 35 is more apt to have a Downs Syndrome child has, in recent times, been contested! On the contrary; a child born into the family as a latecomer has more often proven to be an enrichment to the whole family.

A woman knows she has reached menopause (cessation of menses) when she has not had a menstrual period for at least a year. Before this final period, she will go through the premenopause, which is basically a period of change and is called the climacteric, or change of life. During this time, the remaining egg follicles in the ovary begin to disappear, so that the normal ovarian activity of the reproductive years unwinds gradually and becomes relatively inactive. This means that the lining of the uterus is less stimulated, which in turn causes the menstrual flow to become less regular and predictable. The controlling glands are going into low gear, as they prepare for a quieter phase of life, when the uterus is resting because its special task is completed.

This transition usually takes place between the 45th to 55th year of a woman's life. Just as each of us has a different thumbprint—unique and individual—so every woman has an individual cycle pattern. (Think of the myth of the 28-day cycle; less than 11 percent of women have 28-day cycles!) This means that her period of premenopause will also be different. Some women (probably two-thirds) won't have any difficulties at all. Others can have hot flashes, insomnia, headaches, and skin changes. Some may develop heavy bleeding episodes because of sudden surges of estrogen, followed by long intervals when the menstrual periods are absent. This time of hormonal upheaval is very similar to that which occurred at puberty.

Many women are overcome by extreme tiredness. There are three periods of life when a woman is especially tired: during puberty, during the first three months of pregnancy, and during premenopause. I recently received the following letter from a reader of *The Joy of Being a Woman.*

Dear Mrs. Trobisch,

Thank you for the final chapter of your book, "Menopause—Chance for a New Beginning." It was written just for us, because we are now in this new beginning. But I have a question about the premenopause. Lately I get so tired that I can't do half as much as I used to. I felt the same way when I was a teenager. At that time, I asked my physician if there was something wrong with me. Could my present fatigue be related to what I experienced then? It would be nice if I didn't have to worry about it.

MRS. G.

December 4

Dear Mrs. G.,

The fatigue and loss of energy that you experience are definitely related to the premenopause. Try to be patient with yourself. This phase of your life won't last forever. It is important to see your physician regularly and to try to get at least an extra hour of rest each day. The premenopause is adolescence in reverse.

Think about the image used by Dr. Vollman to characterize a woman's reproductive lifetime: adolescence (a time of rising fertility), maturity (a plateau, the years of optimum fertility), the premenopause or climacteric (a time of declining fertility).

Illustration 4

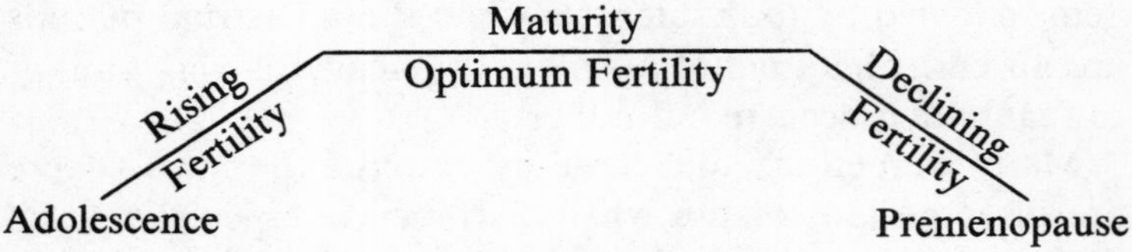

A woman's fertility gradually declines during the premenopause. Only about 1 in 10,000 women are able to conceive at age 47. The changes that occur during the climacteric vary from women to women. The mucus symptom may appear from time to time briefly and then disappear; the temperature rise may be very gradual; or there may be no temperature rise at all during the cycle. At such times, the mucus observation can be of great value. If a woman has learned to identify the sensation of true dryness, then she may consider all the truly dry and interim days, up until the first appearance of mucus, to be infertile.

INGRID TROBISCH

February 7

Dear Dr. Roetzer,

I am 43 years old, and my doctor says that I should not have any more children. I am in agreement with your method, and we have chosen to use the completely infertile time after ovulation. But my cycles are getting very irregular.

I do not wish to take medication to regulate my cycles. Unfortunately, the high-temperature phase now lasts only a few days—sometimes not even one day is available for intercourse.

It seems that during the premenopause, the time of ovulation is delayed until later and later in the cycle. I hardly ever notice intermenstrual pain or the special discharge. So, I'm completely dependent on the temperature pattern. Because I frequently have only a few days in the cycle available for intercourse, I would like to be able to use them fully. The temperature rise is not always clearly identifiable, so I'm quite concerned about what to do.

MRS. R.

March 13

Dear Mrs. R.,

Temperature interpretation is often difficult during the premenopause. At this time in your life, I would like to recommend that you learn to make detailed observations of your mucus symptom (that is, of the cervical mucus secretion). The two enclosed sheets of guidelines contain the essential information you will need to make these observations.

Learning to make exact observations of the cervical mucus is a gradual process; it takes time—usually a few months. I am quite willing to review your charts and return them to you with my comments. I would appreciate it if you would send me all your previous charts.

Interestingly enough, the same rules hold for the premenopause as for the time after childbirth, but there is a difference. During the premenopause, the mucus symptom is noticed less frequently and more sporadically; sometimes bleeding occurs without a preceding high-temperature phase or with only a very short preceding high-temperature phase.

I would like to point out that in other countries, many

women have been able to get along very well during the premenopause solely on the basis of their observations of the mucus symptom. When the symptom is the same, day after day—no change in the mucus observed—it is a sign of infertility. I get letter after letter from women who have learned to make exact mucus observations and then begun to understand their own bodies as a marvelous creation fashioned by God.

DR. ROETZER

Experience of Love; Dialogue in Depth

As you can see from these letters, the time of premenopause can be a difficult time for those who want to have the experience of love that comes with understanding natural family planning. But difficulties are there to be surmounted. We have observed, over and over again, how couples have grown in their relationship, simply by accepting this fact and taking one day at a time. Someone has coined the term *creative snuggling*. To hold and to be held are enriching experiences, and blessed are the couples who have learned this art. During the premenopause, just as during the period of breast-feeding when waiting for the return of fertility, there can be long periods of abstinence—not from love, but perhaps from the genital expression of love.

Frank Wessling has said in his article, "Is It Immature Loving?": "If a husband and wife have not learned in a few years how to give themselves to each other totally in the intimacy of an understood look, they had better get busy learning how to love each other. They are simply lousy lovers. And I don't care if they hustle off to bed every night of the week for the so-called marital embrace. If that is the only lovemaking they do, they are at best only half-alive."

A couple practicing natural family planning learns the secret of dialogue and avoids that pitfall that Esther Harding describes in her book *The Way of All Women:*

When difficulties, no matter what their nature, arise between husband and wife, the temptation to withdraw temporarily from the intimacy and to fly somewhere else inevitably obtrudes itself on consciousness. The woman longs to carry her troubles to her nearest woman friend for sympathy and comfort because her greatest need is on the feeling side and it takes an act of conscious determination to stay and work on the problem with her husband. The man is tempted to fling off and seek out another woman in order to find his sexual satisfaction in a temporary affair where the conditions are not so difficult, but where his obligation can be met by some material gift and where, above all, *no intolerable demand is made to talk things over and to understand.*

John and Sheila Kippley, founders of the Couple to Couple League, have a beautiful chapter in their book *The Art of Natural Family Planning* on the theme of marriage building with NFP. They say:

Periodic abstinence is good for the marriage relationship because it helps avoid the feeling of sexual satiation, the feeling of having too much quantity and a corresponding lack of joy and meaning. . . . Once the couple resumes intercourse, it is a common experience for them to have a heightened appreciation of it. This has led to the saying among some couples who practice NFP, "Every cycle has a period of courtship followed by a honeymoon." There is no universal recipe for the periodic courtship-without-coitus phase of marriage. An excellent exercise in marital communication would be a discussion of what each might do for the other in such periods. The important thing is that they still show each other that they care and are friends. In this way they can actively work against one of the worst enemies of the marital relationship—taking each other for granted. It is a frequent comment that NFP demands a certain amount of maturity to begin with, but results in an even more mature, stable, and happy marital relationship. Repeatedly we have been told by others that the efforts involved in NFP have been repaid tenfold in marriage enrichment.

A Change of Life, Not a Loss

While a man remains fertile all his life, a woman in her premenopause is experiencing a decline in her fertility, until it tapers off altogether. At this time, she has the opportunity of entering a new phase in her life. Her cyclic ups and downs begin to level out. After menopause, she is able to count on herself in a new and different way. Often she enjoys excellent health. A teacher friend of mine testified that since menopause, she had not had to miss a day of school for ten years for health reasons. The afternoon of life is just as full of meaning as the morning; only its meaning and purpose are different. Just as earlier years were given to childbearing and raising, so later years can be used to bring to birth a spiritual creation.

"He who lives well, looks well." The importance of a balanced diet cannot be stressed enough. Many women would find their cycles becoming more regular if they were more careful about their eating and sleeping habits. It is also a time of finally accepting yourself as you are—of standing up to the figure you have, to your age—yes, even to your wrinkles. Aren't they the shorthand of your life? Why should you try to erase or camouflage them? Erik Erikson speaks of late adulthood as "ego integrity or the basic acceptance of one's life as having been meaningful." These middle years are bonus years and offer us a time to reorder our lives, to begin to live differently, so at the end of life we shall be able to look back with satisfaction and be ready to die with peace and serenity.

> Grow old along with me!
> The best is yet to be,
> The last of life, for which the first was made.
> Our times are in his hand.
>
> ROBERT BROWNING

Dr. Hanna Klaus describes the changes that take place in the *Reader in Natural Planning.* As a well-known gynecologist who has had this experience, she is equipped to say:

> Pre-menopause is puberty in reverse. Just as the woman who is beginning to grow into womanhood learns to understand herself in terms of her newly active hormonal picture, putting it all together; so now we're on the other end of the spectrum. And it's coming down.
>
> There are two distinct components to the menopause: the loss of ovulation, which is of course self-evident; it is usually a gradual decline; and the loss of the ovarian cycle hormones. There will be some estrogen coming from the adrenal glands for a while, but this cycle of estrogen followed by progesterone secreted by the ovaries is no longer regular. But along with this there is the loss of reproductive capacity, the heart of a woman's personality. . . .
>
> Nature prepares us for this usually in a 2 or 3 year period when the cycles change. As the level of the ovarian hormone gets a little bit lower, one notices among other things a rise in pre-menstrual tension. It is explained probably by the fact that a woman's adrenals have a fairly regular output of a given amount of the hormone testosterone per day and that this usually insignificant amount of male hormone becomes important when there is an inadequate amount of estrogen and progesterone to oppose it. The result is aggressiveness.

One 58-year-old woman expressed it this way: "My experience of the premenopause was positive. Finally my cycles stopped. I felt more energetic than ever before and began to take seriously my manifold responsibilities in my family, my church, and volunteer work in the hospital. I enjoyed it all. When I meet old friends, the first thing they usually say is, 'You haven't aged a bit!' "

This was a woman who had learned to accept herself, who liked what she saw in the mirror. Another woman may have found her identity in her uterus and during the change of life became devastated at the thought of not being able to have any more children—even though objectively she knew that a woman in her middle years is not as gifted to have children as a woman in her twenties and thirties. Such women can be comforted by the thought of having grandchildren—a very special blessing of the Lord. As the Psalmist prays in Psalms 128:6 RSV: "May you see your children's children. . . ." Life has now come full circle. "Being grandparents is the only stage of life there's nothing wrong with," one couple told us.

Hysterectomy and Mastectomy

Many women must, for medical reasons, have their uterus or breast removed. It can be a traumatic experience, and is a problem for which there is no easy solution. Again, in acceptance lieth peace, though it takes courage and dignity on the part of the woman.

A hysterectomy eliminates the possibility of cancer of the reproductive organs, and so may be considered a blessing for the future. Despite removal of the uterus, marital intercourse in all its fullness can still take place.

In the allegory of the vine and the branches (John 15), Jesus says something from which women who have undergone a hysterectomy or mastectomy can draw consolation: Sometimes God prunes a branch on one part of the vine so that the other parts can bear more abundant fruit. She who is now barren can become fruitful in a entirely different fashion.

One of the ways she can bear fruit is to be a "Doula": one who mothers the mother. This is one of the greatest needs of our society—to provide support for younger mothers, so they can come up for air once in a while and can be acknowledged in the greatness of their ministry as wives and mothers. An older father can be a very good "Doula" too, and will find his life enriched by being a father to the father, as well as to the young mother.

"We've Never Enjoyed It More"

Recently, on one of our teaching tours, we comforted a highly respected African pastor and his wife. She wept bitterly and told us that now that her menopause had taken place and she could no longer have children, she thought she could no longer sleep with her husband. How relieved they both were, to know that menopause and the fact that she could have no more children had nothing to do with their sexual relationship, which could now be more fulfilling than ever.

My husband and I were once invited to speak at a Christian men's conference in Germany, which had as its theme: How to be a good father. In my talk, I stressed the thought that if you want to love your children, you must love the mother of your children. I spoke quite frankly about the importance of harmony in marital relations as well as understanding your fertility as a couple. Later, at the lunch table, I overheard the following conversation between a young father, age thirty, and an elderly gentleman of sixty-five:

"I can imagine," the young man said, "that when you get to be around forty, your sex life is over."

The elderly man stopped eating, looked at him in amazement, and said in no uncertain tones, "That's what *you* might think, my friend. As far as my wife and I are concerned, we've never enjoyed it more!" Life is a passage. Certain doors close; other doors open. Marriage is not only a physical experience of love, but also an emotional and spiritual experience. After facing the tidal ebb and flow of premenopause fertility and infertility, the couple is now ready for the next challenge when fertility ceases completely. With this challenge comes the opportunity for further exploration and enrichment of the emotional and spiritual aspects of the marriage relationship.

A Final Word

We congratulate you who have read these letters and could perhaps identify with one or the other of the writers. Once more may we say: Natural family planning is not a contraceptive method, but a *way of life.* It means to live one day at a time. In the Lord's Prayer, we pray, "Give us *this day* our *daily bread.*" In his explanation of this petition, Martin Luther writes: "What is meant by daily bread? Everything that belongs to the support and wants of the body . . . food, drink, clothing . . . peace, health, discipline . . . We are to say *this day* because we should be satisfied with what we need each day, and because it is *foolish* and *sinful* to worry about the future." We believe that it is possible for a couple to determine whether "this day" is a fertile or infertile day for them and to make their decisions accordingly. Periods of fasting, followed by celebrations and feasts, keep life from becoming monotonous. To learn to enjoy the sacrament of the present moment is a great art.

Basic marital problems are not solved by natural family planning. The goal of marriage is, "Not to be happy, but to make happy; not to be understood, but to understand." If the spouses are willing to get involved in the dialogue that is necessary in order to practice natural family planning successfully, this can be the beginning of the healing process in a troubled marriage. Every day is a new beginning.

"Marriage is starting to love over and over again" says Ulrich Schaffer in his book *A Growing Love.* Because we believe that natural family planning is a marriage-enriching process in which husbands and wives are considered as creatures of God—called and empowered to respond to the divine order of creation—we have written this book. As you make the effort to understand natural family planning, we believe you will have a growing experience of love.

Wishing you joy and peace as you grow together,

ELISABETH ROETZER and INGRID TROBISCH

Appendix A

Evaluating the Waking Temperature in Conjunction with the Mucus Symptom

The material in this appendix is compiled with the permission of Dr. Josef Roetzer, who uses the enclosed guidelines in his advisory service.

This appendix will not be able to answer every question the reader may have. A systematic presentation of natural conception regulation and directions for self-instruction are contained in Dr. Josef Roetzer's book *Family Planning the Natural Way.* Anyone wishing to learn and practice natural family planning successfully on her own will need to read Dr. Roetzer's book.

The Basic Sympto-Thermal Rule: Look for 3 After Peak Higher Than 6

That is, look for 3 consecutive days of "higher" temperature readings, all of which lie **after peak** and all of which are *higher* than the highest of the preceding *6* temperature readings. The completely infertile time of the cycle begins with *evening* on the day of the *3rd* such higher reading, *provided* the 3rd higher reading reaches a certain elevation above the 6 preceding lower readings. To be specific:

1. **The most important rule: Encircle as "higher" readings only those elevated temperature readings which occur after peak day.**

No elevated reading may be encircled if it occurs while the "glassy," "egg-white," "more-fertile-type" mucus is still present. If more-fertile-type mucus cannot be observed, but only the **less**-fertile-type mucus, then you must wait until after the final day of the less-fertile-type mucus before you are allowed to encircle any elevated readings as "higher" readings. If you are **unable** to observe any form of mucus at all, you must wait for 4 readings higher than 6: 4 consecutive readings, each higher than all of the 6 temperature readings preceding the first of those 4.

2. Even if there is a delay in temperature rise after peak, for greatest security, wait for **3** consecutive elevated readings to occur **after** peak day (*see* number 15 below).

3. Furthermore, the **3rd** encircled reading must be at least .36 ° F. (.2 ° C.) higher than the highest of the final 6 low readings.

4. If the encircled **3rd** "higher" reading is not sufficiently elevated, wait until evening on the 4th day of "higher" readings, before assuming infertility. In such a case, the 4th "higher" reading need only be noticeably higher than the 6 lower readings preceding the first "higher" reading. **Note:** It is not possible to tell for certain whether or not you are in the completely infertile time unless you take your waking temperature.

5. Once the requirements of the basic sympto-thermal rule have been met, infertility may be assumed at all times until the end of the cycle, and, with rare exceptions, until midnight at the end of Day 6 of the following cycle.

Infertility at the Beginning of the Cycle

1. The first day of menstruation is the first day of the cycle (Cycle Day 1). **Cycle Days 1–6 are infertile.** (For the extremely rare exceptions to this rule, see p. 16).

2. **During the days following menstruation,** checking for what can be observed at the vaginal entrance is **more important** than taking the waking temperature.

3. **During the days following menstruation,** checking for mucus must be done on each visit to the bathroom. In addition, you must pay attention during the course of the day to the various possible sensations that may present themselves at the vaginal entrance. If, for instance, you suddenly feel as if you are secreting moisture, whereas before you did not, go at once to check by tissue, to see whether there is anything to see on the paper. (*See* chart 45 below, regarding the mere *feeling* of moistness before any secretion appears on the tissue.)

CHART 45

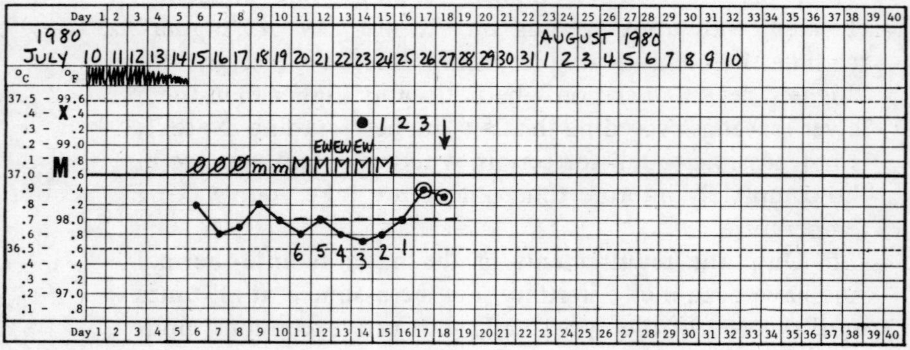

4. In order to avoid confusion, the beginner should take care not to place her fingers inside the vagina itself, which is always rather moist.

5. At first, all mucus observations are to be made only at the **entrance** to the vagina and recorded on the thick middle line for 98.6 ° F/37.0 ° C on the chart. Also, you are to record on the thick middle line *only* the observations that are made externally, at the vaginal entrance.

6. **As soon as the menstrual flow has dwindled significantly or ceased,** you must decide at the **end of each day:**

A. Whether the day was a "dry" day. This means a real feeling of dryness at the vaginal opening, often connected with an unpleasant, itchy feeling. If so, then record a **d** on the chart for the day observed.

B. If you felt uncertain about calling it a "dry" day, and yet there was no feeling of "secreting moisture" and no visible mucus on the tissue, then record a ∅. This stands for "nothing," and we call it the interim.

C. A feeling of "secreting moisture" that was not previously observed is charted with the small letter **m.** This moisture is felt, but does not appear on the tissue.

D. If you observed an increased mucus secretion, then record an **M** (for mucus) on the day observed.

- If the mucus symptom observed looks like **raw egg-white** (usually thin, clear, or cloudy, and in any case stretchy), or if it can be described as **glassy,** write **EW** or **gl** just above the **M** on your chart for that day. If there is *any feeling of slipperiness* (lubrication), or if the *tissue glides easily* over the vaginal opening as a result of any slippery, wet secretion there, note this on your chart; it always means that more-fertile-type mucus is present. **Clear, stretchy, slippery**—any one or more of these traits means more-fertile-type mucus is present.
- "Egg-white" or "glassy" mucus is the typical **more-fertile-type mucus.** Before and after the more-fertile-type mucus appears, another type of mucus is often observed. This other type of mucus is known as **less-fer-**

tile-type mucus. Women have described this particular mucus as being cloudy, white, milky white, or yellow (opaque); thick, lumpy, or creamy; sticky; having little or no stretchability.

7. **Until you are skilled in self-observation, do not assume any days beyond Cycle Day 6 to be infertile.** Whether or not a woman may assume additional days beyond the 6th day of the cycle to be infertile is best clarified by reading the book *Family Planning the Natural Way.* The book is designed for self-instruction. Consultation with an experienced instructor of natural family planning or a visit to a natural-family-planning clinic is also recommended.

- Whether or not a woman may assume infertile days up until the start of noticeable mucus secretion depends upon her **individual pattern** of transition from the dry days to the mucus days and upon the general pattern of her previous cycles. Successful utilization of the infertile days following the menstrual period requires a good knowledge of the female cycle, as well as sufficient personal experience observing and charting one's signs.

8. The **peak day** of an episode of mucus is the **final day** of more-fertile-type mucus during that episode (or the final day of any mucus, in an episode containing only less-fertile-type mucus).

- In an episode containing more-fertile-type mucus it is the final day of the "glassy," "egg-white," "more-fertile-type" mucus that is the peak. This may or may not be the day the mucus is most abundant.
- You know you are not past peak in a mucus episode as long as there is any feeling of **lubrication** still present. Lubrication is the **slippery, wet feeling caused by the more-fertile-type mucus.** This may become so thin and runny that the key to noticing it is the easy tissue glide when wiping or the awareness of slipperiness at the vaginal entrance. Understanding and paying attention to

lubrication is crucial to correct identification of the peak day in a mucus episode. Whenever more-fertile-type mucus is present, the feeling of lubrication is usually also present.

- If the more-fertile-type mucus stops and then resumes within 3 days, the final day of this new appearance of more-fertile-type mucus—even if there is only one day of it—must be considered the peak. The peak of the episode is finally identified when for three days, more-fertile-type mucus has failed to appear. **Note:** After a patch with only less-fertile-type mucus, there must be 3 days in a row of **d** or ∅ before you call the final day of **M** peak.

9. As soon as the peak day of a mucus episode has been identified, mark a large round dot (•) on the chart above the abbreviated entry for the mucus observation of that day (on chart 45, peak day • is Day 14).

10. The basic sympto-thermal rule requires 3 "higher" readings **after** peak, that are higher than the preceding 6 temperatures. There are cycles in which these 3 encircled "higher" readings lie immediately after peak days. In such a case, the onset of the completely infertile time may safely be presumed with evening on the 3rd day after peak.

- Self-observation of the cervical mucus must continue during these 3 days of elevated temperature, however, to make certain that you are past the peak; that is, you must verify that more-fertile-type mucus does not resume during these 3 days (or, in the event that only less-fertile-type mucus was observed, you must verify that the mucus does not begin again).

11. If 3 "higher" readings do not occur on the first 3 days after peak day, then you cannot yet assume any infertility. Instead, the numbers *1, 2, 3* should be entered on the chart after the large dot (•) that signifies the peak of the episode. The combination • *1, 2, 3* means that all 3 days immediately following peak day must be considered fertile **(peak rule).**

12. Beginning with the evening on the 4th day after peak (see arrow on chart 45, on Day 18), infertility may be assumed with a high degree of reliability (**peak rule**). But without 3 days of sustained "higher" readings after peak, the reliability is not as great as if you knew for certain that you were in the completely infertile time.

- In the absence of an established post-peak high-temperature phase, **continued self-observation is necessary, and when mucus begins again, fertility is again assumed.**

13. Among women who are skilled in self-observation of mucus symptom, the **peak rule** has proven very successful, particularly during the time after delivery, when totally breast-feeding, and during the change of life, when long intervals without temperature shift may occur (these are two periods of overall lower fertility in a woman's reproductive life). In the author's own advisory service, observance of the **peak rule** outlined above has never resulted in pregnancy during postpartum and premenopause.

14. The peak rule is also helpful in cycles in which 3 consecutive "higher" readings cannot be identified according to the criteria given above in "The Basic Sympto-Thermal Rule," or when the "higher" readings appear only somewhat later than peak day.

15. During the years that are normally fertile, a woman may assume infertility beginning with evening on the 4th day after the peak of a mucus episode only if the waking temperature shows at least a noticeable rising trend. Nevertheless, the reliability of such a rule is not as great as if you knew for certain that you were in the completely infertile time.

- In the following chart, the numbers *1, 2, 3* after the peak and an arrow on the 4th day after the peak illustrate the decision-making situation a couple may find themselves in. The arrow indicates that on the 4th day past the peak, the couple must decide whether the temperature pattern suggests infertility or not, assuming that the rise is somewhat delayed after peak. On this chart, the 4th day past the peak reveals 2 "higher" readings, in what might (or might not) continue as the sustained high-temperature phase. With this combination—peak plus 4 *and* 2 "higher" readings—it would be an extremely rare event, should intercourse at the end of the 4th day after peak result in pregnancy. In my own advisory service, I have seen no pregnancy result from intercourse on the 5th day after peak, with the combination: Peak plus 5 *and* 2 "higher" readings.

Chart 45

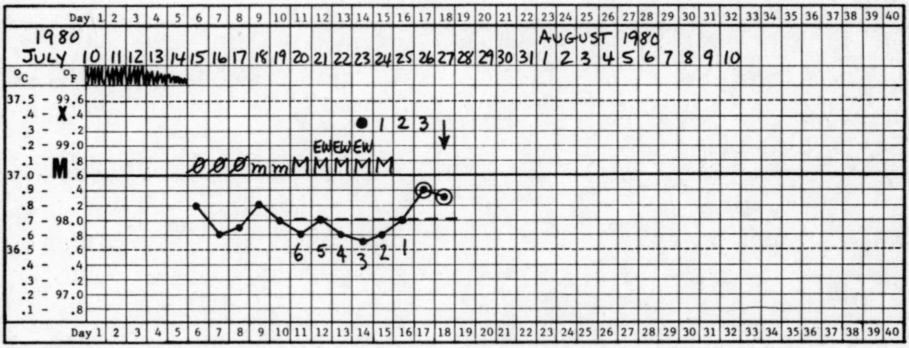

In the above chart, the broken line running through the highest of the final 6 lower readings must be drawn, before attempting to identify "higher" readings. After a little practice, it becomes easy to recognize within almost any temperature pattern where the series of elevated readings begin that are higher than the preceding 6. The only elevated readings that may be encircled as **higher** readings are those that lie **after** peak. **m** = a feeling of "secreting moisture" that previously was not present, *and* there is nothing at all yet on the tissue.

- Women who have dry (**d**) or interim (∅) days after menstruation and who, prior to any visible mucus on the tissue, are able to notice this **mere feeling of moistness** (charted **m**), can presume with a high degree of probability that all the **d** or ∅ days prior to **m** are infertile. We do need more experience before presenting this as a reliable rule, however.

18. The conclusions of my experience may be summarized as follows: For greatest security, wait for 3 consecutive elevated readings to occur *after* peak day, before assuming completely infertile time.

Appendix B

Natural Family Planning During the Postpartum

1. Begin charting mucus and temperature observations **3 weeks after delivery.**

- During the postpartum, it is more important to check for mucus than to take your waking temperature. Each day enter a **d** or ∅ or **M** on your chart, starting from Cycle Day 21 after delivery, even though at first you do not take your temperature or do not take it every day.
- Do not wait until your menstrual period returns before starting to chart mucus and temperature observations. It is possible for fertility to return and for conception to occur without a previous menstrual period.

2. From the begining of the **4th week after** a normal delivery there are, generally speaking, no medical objections to resumed intercourse.

3. **The first 6 weeks after** delivery are infertile, even for the nonbreast-feeding mother. If you are totally breast-feeding, there will be more than 6 weeks of infertility. These infertile weeks after delivery permit a couple to enjoy marital relations without anxiety and without undue waiting after the birth of their child.

- It is doubtful whether conception can occur during the 7th week postpartum. In any case, a woman may safely assume infertile days during the 7th week postpartum and thereafter, provided that neither the typical "egg-white" or "glassy" mucus (the "more-fertile-type mucus"), or the other type of mucus that may normally precede it, is present. After even a single day of "egg-white" or "glassy" mucus, the immediately following 3 days must be considered fertile (**peak rule**). During the postpartum, infertility may be assumed beginning with the 4th day after the peak of a mucus episode. Should the mucus reappear on the 4th day after the peak of a mucus episode, or later, then a woman must of course consider herself again possibly fertile.
- When a woman is not breast-feeding, normal cycling usually returns very quickly, starting with the 7th week after delivery. Most often there is a short high-temperature phase prior to the first true menstruation after delivery, with some form of **M** preceding the temperature rise.

4. **When a woman totally breast-feeds,** there is infertility for at least 12 weeks after delivery. **Total breast-feeding** means that the baby is nursed on demand as long as it wishes to suckle and receives absolutely no supplements but receives everything from the breast and is breast-fed during the night. The baby's sole pacifier must be the mother's breast. A Vitamin-D supplement is in most cases unnecessary; breast milk contains all the Vitamin D the baby needs.

- Mucus (**M**) may periodically appear and then disappear, without being associated with ovulation. A temperature rise may or may not follow a mucus episode.
- If a woman observes the rules for evaluating episodes of mucus in the absence of a temperature rise, following the peak rule, she will be able to determine infertility

after each mucus episode (the peak rule is highly reliable during the time of breast-feeding after childbirth) beyond the first 12 weeks postpartum. Important details regarding proper application of the peak rule are contained in *Family Planning the Natural Way.*

- Any days of **bleeding not preceded by a high-temperature phase** are treated as if they were days of **M,** and the final day of such bleeding is treated as the peak day of a mucus episode. In other words, **no infertility** is to be assumed during the bleeding or for three days afterward; these must be **d** or ∅ days. If mucus is present when the bleeding stops, then, of course, apply the peak rule after the mucus.
- Some women who totally breast-feed experience no bleeding for 6 months or even longer after delivery. For such women there is absolutely no need to induce menses (such a procedure is, in fact, contraindicated). On occasion, a totally breast-feeding mother will experience no signs of fertility for 6 months or longer, and some remain infertile for a year or more after delivery.
- The period of total breast-feeding represents a time of at least a sharply lowered overall level of fertility. The peak rule is therefore highly reliable when the woman totally breast-feeds. The peak rule remains reliable even after supplements have been introduced; but once a woman has had her first postpartum true menstruation, the rules for normal cycling apply (*see* Appendix A).

Self-examination of the cervix can be particularly helpful, especially when any continuous discharge or continuous moistness is the pattern.

5. **As soon as three post-peak "higher" temperature readings are** observed and encircled in the usual fashion, infertility may be assumed, as during normal cycling. But the following must also be kept in mind: During the postpartum

months, you should continue to take the waking temperature daily. The continuation of the high-temperature phase assures you of the continuation of infertility. When the temperature readings drop back to the low level, your judgment of fertility or infertility would again have to be based on the results of self-observation at the vaginal entrance or at the cervix.

- The high-temperature phase may be shorter and less pronounced than usual for the first few cycles postpartum.

Natural Family Planning During the Premenopause

During premenopause, follow the same rules regarding episodes of mucus, episodes of bleeding, and temperature pattern as during total breast-feeding.